THE CHARMER

Nicola Marsh

*Ariel Wallace is a free spirit who will do anything to save her art gallery.
Well, almost anything...*

Cooper Vance, a hotshot property developer, has his sights on Ariel's gallery and when he's mistaken for a life-portrait model...who wouldn't take advantage of that?

Cooper has a steadfast rule to never mix business with pleasure...but with the intriguing artist calling his bluff at every turn, maybe it's time to become a rule-breaker?

Copyright © Nicola Marsh 2021
Published by Parlance Press 2024

All the characters, names, places and incidents in this book have no existence outside the imagination of the author and have no relation whatsoever to anyone bearing the same name or names and are used fictitiously. They're not distantly inspired by any individual known or unknown to the author and all the incidents in the book are pure invention. Any resemblance to actual events, locales, or persons, living or dead, is coincidental.

All rights reserved including the right of reproduction in any form. The text or any part of the publication may not be reproduced or transmitted in any form without the written permission of the publisher.

The author acknowledges the copyrighted or trademarked status and trademark owners of the word marks mentioned in this work of fiction.

First Published by Harlequin Enterprises in 2010 as BIG-SHOT BACHELOR and MISTRESS TO THE TYCOON.
World English Rights Copyright © 2020 Nicola Marsh

Chapter One

"Come in and take off all your clothes."

Ariel Wallace grimaced at how forward that sounded and mentally rehearsed another spiel.

"Make your way out the back. You'll find pegs to hang your clothes on."

That sounded worse.

"You've probably done this a thousand times before so head through that door, disrobe, and let's get started."

No way.

Ariel shook her head and covered her face with her hands, not surprised to feel heat scorching her cheeks and deriving little comfort from the familiar smell of turpentine on her paint-splotched skin.

She couldn't do this.

Being an artist involved spontaneous bursts of creativity, fabulous blending of colours, and frantic slashes of brushes, not inviting some guy she didn't know to take his clothes off so she could paint him.

Whopping big profit or not.

She'd find some other way to keep *Colour by Dreams*

afloat. She had to. She'd promised Aunt Barb, the founder of this amazing gallery and the woman who had practically raised her, that her legacy would live on.

Ariel would do anything to make that happen.

The soft tinkle of wind chimes signalled a visitor entering the gallery and Ariel stiffened, her hands lowering from her face as she braced for an awkward confrontation. She knew how much uni students needed money and giving some poor guy the brush-off, no pun intended, didn't sit well with her.

If anyone knew about being poor, she did.

Which is exactly why she had to paint her first life portrait since art school.

She had no choice.

"Hello? Anyone here?"

"Be there in a second," she called out, casting a final longing look at the back door, wishing she could make a quick dash for it.

Instead, she smoothed her favourite ochre peasant skirt, retied the paisley bandanna under her unruly curls, and schooled her face into an *'I'm in charge and not in the mood for nonsense'* expression before stepping through the beaded curtain that separated her work area from the gallery out front.

"Miss Wallace? I'm Cooper—"

"Hi, Cooper. My studio's in the back, so if you head out there, I'll lock up here and be with you shortly."

The words tumbled out in a rush, a combination of nerves and shock. She'd expected a lean, young, scruffy guy to come slinking into the gallery looking half as embarrassed as she felt. Instead, she struggled not to stare at Cooper. She had no interest in his surname; she didn't want to get too personal considering she'd soon be seeing him in the buff.

THE CHARMER

Naked...

She swallowed, unable to link buff and naked with the guy standing in front of her. If she'd been mortified at painting some dishevelled, half-starved student without his clothes on, the thought of Cooper—all six-three, broad shoulders, long legs, killer smile, too-blue eyes, and dark hair—sitting for her without a stitch of clothing made her light-headed.

Though she could blame that on the oil paint fumes.

"I wasn't sure you'd want to do this," he said, amusement lighting his eyes, making them sparkle in the muted lights and sending an unexpected bolt of awareness through her.

"I have no choice."

She stared, stunned by his easy confidence, his cool poise. Wasn't this guy the teensiest bit embarrassed about getting naked in front of a stranger?

By his cocky grin and casual stance, obviously not.

"We always have a choice, Miss Wallace," he said, his deep voice resounding in the high-ceilinged room, as sexy as the rest of him.

Damn it, and that was with his clothes on.

It had been way too long since she'd been on a date. She definitely had to get out more if scoping out the models, a routine aspect of her work, had her practically swooning.

"Actually, I don't have a choice. If I can't capture you on canvas and sell the painting for the fortune I've been promised, I lose this place to some slime-ball developers who've been buying up the rest of this street."

Confusion clouded his eyes for a second before a tiny frown creased his brow and his smile vanished.

Great, she was scaring off prime model material before she'd even started.

Blowing a stray curl out of her eyes, she said, "Sorry to dump all that on you. I tend to babble when I'm nervous and to be honest, I haven't done nudes in quite a while. Guess I'm a bit bashful."

She averted her eyes and crossed the room, her beaded flip-flops slapping noisily against the polished Tasmanian oak boards, not wanting to see him staring at her as if she had two heads. Or worse, laughing at her. She'd always hated being laughed at, something the kids she grew up with at the orphanage soon learned.

"You think I'm here to model?"

After locking the door and flipping the sign to 'closed', she swung back to face him, wishing she didn't need the money so desperately. Nothing was worth this awkward tenseness, even if he was the first guy to capture her attention in a long while.

"Aren't you?"

Her gaze flicked over him, starting at his almost-black hair worn a tad too long and curling at the collar of his navy polo shirt, over the snug way the shirt's cotton moulded his impressive chest, and downwards, where faded denim encased long, lean legs.

No doubt about it. Perfect model material, and he would be incredible to paint if those muscles hinted at beneath his clothes were as impressive as she thought. But there was something about him...something off-putting, like he didn't belong here.

He paused, staring at her too intently as if making up his mind about something. Well, she would have to make it up for him. She didn't have all night and as much as she didn't want to do this, the sooner they made a start the better.

"Look, I know this is awkward for both of us. Why don't

we head out the back and I make us a nice cup of honey and ginger tea? It'll help us relax."

Unlikely, because how discombobulated this guy made her feel, she'd need to drink five kettle's worth to calm the hell down. "You can get changed behind that screen over there and I'll be back in a minute."

Ariel couldn't fathom the shock in Cooper's blue eyes as she headed into her studio. She expected to hear his footsteps following her and when he didn't move, it hit her.

His confusion, his reticence, his cocky cover-up act: this had to be his first time posing nude. He was probably more nervous than her.

Pausing in the doorway, she turned back to him, hoping to allay some of his discomfort.

"Cooper, if it makes you feel any better, you can keep your underwear on for this sitting," she said, with her best smile, much cheerier now she knew someone else in the room felt more embarrassed about this whole fiasco than she did.

Chapter Two

Cooper didn't move.

He couldn't. He tried but both feet seemed firmly rooted to the spot as he watched the woman float through a curtain of shimmering purple glass beads after sending him a bewitching smile that could make a guy seriously rethink his career.

After all, look at the way his mind was working at the moment. He'd gone from Melbourne's number one property developer to artist's model—*nude* model—in less than a flash of pearly whites set against a luscious rosebud mouth.

He must be losing it.

All those extra hours at *Vance Corporation* trying to make a name for himself must've fried his brain.

This was obviously a silly case of mistaken identity and the sooner he cleared it up, stated his business, secured what he'd come here for, and headed back to the office, the sooner he could launch his dreams.

"Cooper? Tea's ready. Come and get it."

Squaring his shoulders, he pushed through the ridiculous dangling beads in the doorway, getting caught up in the process. After disentangling himself, he stepped into a magical cave.

At least, that's what it appeared to be. In each corner of the large room, swatches of gossamer-thin gold fabric hung from hooks on the ceiling and fell to the floor in cascading waves. Two ruby sofas sat at opposing ends of the room, covered in royal blue and purple cushions. Unlit candles of all sizes, shapes, and colours covered every available surface, while oil paintings of every description covered the walls.

The overall effect, bright, stunning, and welcoming, made him gawk. Though that might have more to do with the gorgeous woman standing in the middle of the eclectic room with a strangely vulnerable smile curving her lush mouth.

"Drink some of this," she said, holding a steaming cup of tea. "It'll make you feel better."

He took the chipped pottery cup she offered, mentally searching for the right words. Maybe he should take a leaf out of her book and opt for brutal honesty? Something to the effect that he was the *'slime ball property developer buying out the street'?*

Yeah, that would go down a treat.

Taking a tentative sip of the pungent brew—a brave move, considering he was a five espressos a day kinda guy and hated the herbal stuff—he tried not to stare at the woman standing between him and his corporation.

"Good?"

"Mmm," he said, surprised he didn't have to lie as the warm honey and spicy ginger slid across his tongue, giving his taste buds a pleasant jolt in the process.

"Drink up, then we can get started."

He tried not to stare, he really did, but there was something about Ariel Wallace that drew his gaze like a connoisseur to a masterpiece.

She wasn't a beauty in the classic sense, what with the crazy flowery bandanna covering her blonde curls, the heart-shaped face devoid of makeup, the pert nose, and wary green eyes that looked like she'd seen more than her fair share of trouble.

As for her body, what little he could see of it beneath a voluminous ruffled skirt that matched her bandanna, and loose white cotton top that hid more than it revealed, he wished he could see more.

He didn't go for boho as a rule, but Ariel's striking face and bizarre dress sense made for an exotic combination, and her unique style had captured his attention. Go figure. He found it particularly strange because he usually admired classically dressed women, the bulk of his female acquaintances preferring classy black and expensive jewellery.

"If you pop behind the screen and get ready, I'll set up over there."

Her brisk, no-nonsense tone had him hiding a smile behind his cup. She could be instructing him to take out the garbage rather than get naked.

Time to set the record straight.

"Miss Wallace, I don't think this is going to work. There's been a mistake—"

"No." She crossed the room in two-seconds flat, standing toe to toe with him before he could blink. "There's no mistake. I haven't got time to find another model. I need this painting done ASAP and that means you're staying, nerves or not. Got it?"

If she jabbed him in the chest, he wouldn't have been surprised.

"And call me Ariel."

THE CHARMER

She stared at him, so close he could see the tiny gold flecks flickering in the green depths of her striking eyes, issuing a challenge he had no intention of taking up.

"I'm not nervous." Though with this crazy woman looking ready to deck him if he refused to take his clothes off, maybe he should be. "I'm not who you think I am."

She quirked an eyebrow, a cheeky elevation that drew his attention to her eyes again, their unusual crystal clear green distracting him from the task at hand: set the record straight, seal this deal, and escape the office, his father, and the memories.

"Look, Cooper, you could be the Crown Prince of Transylvania for all I care. Right now, I need you sitting on that stool without any clothes on, staring out that window, and holding the pose until I say move. Okay?"

"This is insane," he muttered, admiring her sass and wondering if she'd slug him when he told her the truth.

She was close enough to do it. Way too close, considering her intoxicating scent—the faintest hint of jasmine and oranges—was playing havoc with his brain. Because for one, tiny, infinitesimal second, he almost considered doing what she said.

"No, you're insane if you think you're leaving here tonight before I get your form sketched. Now, shelve the shy act and let's get to it."

She cast him one last challenging glare before strutting to an easel about five feet away, busying herself with charcoals and paper to give him time to disrobe.

He must be mad.

Nuts. Crazy. Totally insane.

Then again, considering how desperate he was to obtain this gallery—the last bit of prime real estate in Brunswick Street and his ticket out of *Vance Corporation*—

maybe taking off his clothes for the crazy lady wouldn't be so bad.

"You ready yet?" She asked, without turning around.

"Almost."

With a wry grin, Cooper headed for the ornate Japanese screen, pulling his T-shirt off along the way. As a method to inveigle his way into a client's confidence, he'd never imagined getting naked.

Then again, this wasn't his fault. He'd tried to tell her the truth and she wouldn't listen.

Ariel Wallace wanted a model and it looked like he was it.

He just hoped she wouldn't spear him with the nearest paint brush when she discovered he'd come here to pull the easel out from under her.

Chapter Three

"Don't move."

Ariel picked up her third charcoal nub, tilted her head to get a better view of Cooper's impressive pecs, and let her fingers fly across the paper, hoping to capture some of the model's essence before her aching hand gave out completely.

Easier said than done considering she'd never seen a guy's body like this before; all hard lines, delineated muscles, and large expanses of smooth, tanned skin.

Perfection.

"You've been sketching for an hour and I'm cramping." He winced. "I've got to stretch my legs."

"Oh no, you don't."

She glared at him, determined to get as much from this first sitting as possible. The less she saw of Cooper's buffed body the better and the thought of having to sit through more than a few evenings of seeing his muscles in all their glory made her break out in a cold sweat.

She really needed to get out more.

"You're a hard woman," he muttered, shifting slightly to

the left as light fell across his right shoulder, dappling his upper torso with intriguing shadows.

Magnificent.

If Sofia Montessori, Melbourne's society matriarch wasn't happy with this commission, nothing would satisfy her critical eye.

"I'm a businesswoman. I guess being hard goes with the territory."

She stared at his right clavicle, hoping she could capture the exact angle, not surprised she'd focussed all her attention on his upper body and virtually ignored his bottom half.

Even with Cooper wearing boxer shorts—brief, black, poured-on boxer shorts—and his leg bent, heat flooded her cheeks at the thought of sketching Cooper in his entirety. Having such an impressive model had startled her enough for one night and she couldn't face drawing the whole 'life' aspect of his body in one sitting.

"So you own this place?"

Happy to answer his question—anything to deflect her wandering attention away from those skimpy boxers—she said, "Technically, yes. My aunt opened this gallery years ago and she left it to me when she died. But what with the recent fire in the storeroom, the skyrocketing insurance premiums, and the increasing overheads, it's getting tougher to keep the place open."

Not that she could contemplate closing. She owed Barb, her surrogate aunt, more than she could hope to repay.

"Sorry to hear about your aunt."

Concern flickered across his face and he glanced away, not quite able to meet her eye as a ripple of unease slid down her spine.

Cooper looked almost...guilty? He couldn't be. What

did some guy who didn't know her have to be guilty about? It must be her exhausted mind playing tricks on her. That, and the shock of his gorgeous bod sending her wow-factor off the scale.

"Thanks. Barb was amazing. Just ask anyone along this street."

"Everyone knew her?"

Ariel nodded. "She fostered local talent and more. Barb rarely made a profit, donating huge chunks of money to charities and doing a lot of one-on-one with the street kids in the area."

Like taking in a runaway eight-year-old and giving her a home, something Ariel had never had before. "She was a Brunswick Street icon."

"Sounds like quite a lady."

Touched by the admiration she heard in Cooper's voice, Ariel continued babbling about a subject close to her heart. "That's why this particular portrait is so important to me. I need the cash to keep the gallery open and I need it ASAP, so if I seemed a bit pushy earlier, I'm sorry."

"Chalk it up to the temperamental artist, huh?"

"You got it."

Ariel lifted her gaze from Cooper's shoulder to his face, hearing the gentle teasing in his voice and liking it way too much.

She didn't date much, she didn't socialise a lot. Keeping the gallery open and viable took up all her time and she liked it that way. Work she could rely on; people, rarely.

What was it about this guy that her wishing for something more? Wishing for an easygoing companion at the end of a hard day to listen to her rambling, to give her an encouraging smile when she needed it, to tease her?

"We're done," she said all-too-briskly, snapping shut her

box of charcoals and running a weary hand over her eyes, more to block out the sight of Cooper's body than anything else.

Now that she'd stopped working, seeing him almost naked took on an intimate connotation, when the last thing she wanted or needed was to associate the words 'naked' and 'intimate' with him.

Especially when she had at least another four sittings until she completed the painting.

"Great."

He slid off the stool and she quickly averted her gaze, not wanting to see any more than she had to, sure his butt would be as toned as the rest of him.

"So is it finished?"

"What?"

She sank onto her ergonomic seat, blowing on the annoying curl that consistently fell across her eyes no matter how much she moussed, gelled, or waxed it, relieved he'd popped behind the screen in record time.

"I take it I'm all done here?"

His voice drifted over the screen and she closed her eyes, its rich timbre eliciting visions of smooth whiskey in front of a smouldering fire.

Great. Apart from needing to get out more, maybe she should air the studio better. The paint and turpentine fumes were definitely getting to her.

"You really haven't done this before, have you?"

"Uh...no," he said, emerging from behind the screen, his appeal not diminished in the slightest by clothes.

Especially now she knew exactly what lay beneath.

"Well, let me clue you in. You sit, I sketch, draw, paint, whatever it takes to get this baby done. Tonight, I sketched your basic form but there's a lot more to be done."

THE CHARMER

Like sketch his *whole* form, but she wouldn't think about that right now.

"I don't think—"

"You're not paid to think, you're paid to sit. So, how does tomorrow evening suit you?"

By the pained expression on his handsome face, it looked like he equated having a wisdom tooth extracted without anaesthetic to posing for her again, and she rushed on, not giving him an opportunity to refuse.

"No problems? Good. See you here at seven. You know the way out."

Ariel bolted up the stairs to her apartment, waiting for the front door to shut before sidling down again. After the inane chatter and banter she'd exchanged with Cooper, the gallery's silence seemed almost oppressive.

Sighing, she flicked off the light switches, secured the front door, and headed for the stairs. However, the lure of seeing what she'd achieved tonight pulled her toward her easel. Usually, she preferred to leave her work overnight and appraise it with a fresh eye in the morning, but not tonight.

Maybe it was the unusual subject she'd worked with, maybe it was professional curiosity, but whatever drew her to the myriad sketches she'd done of Cooper, the minute she laid eyes on what she'd captured, she wished she hadn't looked.

Usually modest about her work, she knew what she'd sketched tonight was some of her best work. She'd captured the curve of his jaw, his high cheekbones, the breadth of his chest, and his strong arms, perfectly. Every muscle ripple across his torso, every shaded dip of his waist, she'd managed to transfer his magnificence onto the canvas and she couldn't be happier.

She'd done such a good job she blinked, half expecting the sketch to come to life and step off the paper.

Her chest tightened at the thought of painting Cooper in his entirety and she knew it would take every ounce of her professionalism to view him as a life model and not the first interesting guy to enter her empty life in a long time.

Chapter Four

"How did things go with the Wallace woman? Make any progress with the acquisition?"

Cooper nodded and handed his father a strong, black, sugarless coffee, just the way Eric Vance liked it. "We met. I'm making inroads."

Cooper hid a cynical grin behind his coffee mug, still unable to fathom what had happened last night.

"What's that supposed to mean?" A deep frown marred Eric's brow. "Is she ready to sell? Because that's all I'm interested in, the bottom line. That woman's been the bane of my existence for the last twelve months and if you're not up for the job I'll find someone who is."

His father glowered for extra effect, drank the scalding coffee in one go, yanked his leather director's chair out from behind his desk, and plopped into it, his scowl deepening by the second.

"Rather than scare her off by barging in there, I'm taking a softer approach," *Unlike you*, Cooper thought, but wisely kept that gem to himself.

Thankfully, he was nothing like his dad in the business

arena, precisely why he had to get out of this company, the sooner the better.

"Taking a soft approach is a waste of time," Eric snapped, grabbing the nearest object, which happened to be a gold pen, and tapping it relentlessly against the edge of his desk. "That damn woman is stringing us along, hoping to get more cash out of us."

Cooper stiffened. Though he hardly knew Ariel, she was nothing like the mercenary vulture his dad had made her out to be. From the top of her mussed curls to the bottom of her pale blue painted toenails, she'd appeared genuine, an artist doing it tough but with a clear goal: keep her gallery open in memory of its original owner, a family member.

Seeing her passion for the gallery, hearing her articulate her motivation for not selling, had been honourable, but where did that leave him?

He couldn't weaken, no matter how much he admired Ariel and her convictions. He had dreams of his own to build, starting with obtaining the very property she was trying to save.

"I'm handling it," Cooper said, avoiding his father's assessing stare by striding to the huge glass windows overlooking Flinders Street Station and the Art Centre Spire behind it.

He loved Melbourne, the hip, cosmopolitan feel of the city, the multicultural restaurants, the architecture. He'd acquired and developed many buildings since completing his MBA and each completed deal had brought him immense satisfaction.

Then why the slight niggle that obtaining the last prime piece of real estate in trendy Brunswick Street, Fitzroy, wouldn't be the be-all and end-all he'd first thought?

His father's sinister chuckle didn't reassure him. "You're *handling it*, huh? Well, take as long as you like. I'm not the one who proposed some stupid deal in the first place."

Cooper slowly clenched and unclenched his fists, loathing how his father baited him on a daily basis, hating how their working relationship had come to this.

"We've talked about my plans at length. It's way past time I branched out on my own."

Eric snickered, his disdain obvious. "It's a dumb idea. We can be a team here and when I retire, this whole company is yours."

With Eric a fit fifty-five, retirement would be a long way off, meaning Cooper would be kowtowing to his tyrannical father for the foreseeable future. Unfathomable.

"It's time I left and we both know it."

Eric's eyes narrowed to cold, hard slits, his mutinous expression reminiscent of every time Cooper had disagreed with him since he'd turned ten. "You signed a two year contract when you first started and you've been here less than a year. I could make things tough for you."

Cooper clamped down on the urge to shout. They'd had this same conversation every day for the last week, ever since his dad had failed to buy the gallery for the umpteenth time and Cooper had seized on an idea as his way out.

"Cut the empty threats, Dad. I seal the Brunswick deal, you release me from my contract so I can set up my company. You agreed, remember?"

Eric rolled his eyes, like Cooper was behaving like a petulant child. "Of course I remember. What do you think your old man is, stupid?" He steepled his fingers. "I've had enough of your *brilliant* ideas to last me a lifetime, so why don't you take a seat and bring me up to speed with the Docklands deal."

Gritting his teeth, Cooper turned away from the window and took a seat opposite his dad, who glared at him with perpetual anger. They'd been so close once. Bouncing jokes off each other, getting a kick out of the same stuff: football, old Western films, sailing. The Vance guys on top of their game.

His dad used to laugh a lot back then, thriving on the thrill of an acquisition, sharing his success with him, enjoying a quiet celebratory beer together after work. Fishing holidays, guy weekends-away. Then Cooper had joined the firm and started to forge his own success in the business arena and his dad had changed. Not in a good way.

"The Docklands deal is almost completed," Cooper said. "The contracts are with the legal department as we speak. So once I've got Ariel Wallace's go ahead and I wrap up the Brunswick Street deal, I'm done."

For a second, something akin to anguish flashed in his father's eyes, but before Cooper could fathom it Eric blinked and his dad's latent anger quickly replaced anything Cooper might've imagined.

Eric's upper lip quirked in a sneer. "You'll never make it on your own."

Cooper stood, keeping a tight leash on a host of fiery retorts, and headed for the door and the sanctity of his own office.

"We'll see, Dad. We'll see," he said, more determined than ever to get the deal done with Ariel Wallace.

Chapter Five

"*Ciao, bella.* How's my favourite artist today?"

Sofia Montessori breezed into *Colour by Dreams*, her plump figure swathed in head to toe crimson, making her look like a ripe tomato. Ariel loved colour and Sofia's vibrant wardrobe never failed to brighten her day.

"I'm fine. How's life in the fast lane?"

"I can't complain." Sofia shrugged. "You know how it is. Places to go, people to meet, men to impress."

"Actually, I don't know," Ariel said, bracing for the usual onslaught of Sofia's suffocating hugs and smacking kisses on both cheeks, smiling when she saw the usual matchmaking gleam in Sofia's dark eyes. "And I like it that way."

Sofia threw her hands up in the air and looked toward the heavens. "You are young and beautiful. You should be partying, meeting men your own age, dancing the night away—"

"I'd rather paint the night away." Ariel quickly cut in, knowing that once Sofia got on a roll, she'd be here all day.

"Speaking of which, I started your commission last night. Want to take a look?"

"*Si*. I want to see this life portrait that my sister is so keen on hanging in her house. Can you imagine, a naked man in the dining room?" Sofia tut-tutted. "The thought alone is enough to put me off my ravioli. But it's Maria's fortieth birthday and it's all she's talked about since she visited the National Art Gallery, and what my baby sister wants she shall get."

Sofia rolled her eyes and puffed out her cheeks in disgust and Ariel chuckled at her theatrics, knowing full well the rich Italian woman with a reputation as a connoisseur of younger men was excited about this portrait and would probably order one for herself once she got a look at Ariel's subject.

"I've only done a few preliminary sketches but you'll get the general idea," Ariel said, pushing through the bead curtain leading to her studio and holding it up for Sofia to pass through, slightly nervous about the woman's reaction.

She rarely showed anyone her work before the final canvas, but this was different. Sofia was paying her a small fortune and she didn't want anything to go wrong. She desperately needed the money. Like yesterday.

"The sketches I've done are over here."

Ariel needn't have pointed. She knew the exact moment Sofia laid eyes on the sketches of Cooper.

"Who is *that*?"

"That is the gift you're giving Maria."

Ariel's casual wave of her hand didn't fool Sofia for a second.

"*Bella*, I know what *that* is. I want to know *who* that is."

Ariel laughed at the predatory gleam in Sofia's wide eyes. "The model's name is Cooper. That's all I know."

A lie. She knew a heck of a lot more than that; like the way his blue eyes hid a secret, as if he were ashamed of modelling. And the way his muscles rippled when he moved. And the way his deep voice had made her feel: like a woman who didn't have responsibilities, like a woman who could forget everything after the glimpse of his smile.

Sheesh. She really needed to start wearing a face mask to block the studio fumes from frying her brain.

"*Bellissimo*. This Cooper is gorgeous, no?"

"No. Yes. You know what I mean," Ariel said, turning away from her sketches before her cheeks flushed crimson like Sofia's.

She didn't like admitting how gorgeous Cooper was. She had to remain objective and view him as a means to an end for her work. That's it.

She just hoped she remembered her professional objectivity tonight when she had to sketch his bottom half.

"Is there more to see?" Sofia's eyebrows wiggled suggestively and Ariel knew exactly how much 'more' the older woman wanted to see.

"No, I haven't got to that part yet."

And despite her earlier intention not to blush, heat surged into her cheeks.

Sofia's ear-splitting grin didn't help. "Ah...but I'm sure you're looking forward to it. If that part is as impressive as the rest, we're all in for a treat, no?"

"No."

Sofia cackled and slipped an arm around her shoulders, the heady combination of expensive floral perfume and hairspray tickling Ariel's nose.

"You are a sweet girl, *bambina*. Why won't you accept money from me rather than paint men's rude bits?"

"We've been through this," Ariel said, slipping from

Sofia's claustrophobic embrace and crossing to an open window. "You're a wonderful kind woman but I can't accept your charity. I need to do this on my own."

Sofia clucked and shook her head, sending mushrooms of hair product into the air while her bouffant didn't move a millimetre. "Babs wouldn't want you running yourself into the ground to keep the gallery open. She loved you too much."

"And that's exactly why I have to continue her work. I've got Chelsea Lynch's first show coming up next month, and Chelsea's exactly the type of local talent Barb would've busted a gut for. Chelsea's had a tough life, brought up on the streets around here, and is finally doing something with her life. I need to be there for her, for all of them."

Just like Aunt Barb had been there for her.

What the kind-hearted woman had ever seen in a rebellious eight-year-old street urchin she'd never know, but from the first minute Barb had found her sleeping out the back of the gallery, wrapped in a paint-splattered canvas, Ariel had known nothing but patience and understanding and love. She'd been one of the lucky ones and now it was her turn to give back.

"You are a saint," Sofia said, kissing her fingertips and blowing the kiss toward her.

"At the price I'm charging you for this commission, you think?"

Ariel's gaze drifted toward the sketches of Cooper, wondering if her luck had finally changed when he'd walked in the door last night.

For her, art channelled beauty, and though life portraits came in many shapes and forms she knew that working with a perfect subject like Cooper would do a lot more for her inspiration than painting some recalcitrant, skinny guy.

THE CHARMER

And who knew, with a portrait of a great looking subject like Cooper hanging in the house of one of Melbourne's richest women, she might get inundated with commissions, meaning she could teach more classes, support more shows, and do more for the local charities.

She'd make sure this was her best work, rude bits or not, if it killed her.

"Your work is beautiful, *bambina*. You don't charge nearly enough." Sofia held up a hand when Ariel opened her mouth to refute this. "I will not hear another word. You do this painting for me, we talk some more then. Now, I must go. Antonio is taking me to a divine new trattoria in Lygon Street."

"Who's Antonio?"

"A very sweet boy." Sofia batted her long eyelash extensions and Ariel laughed, knowing Antonio would be young, handsome, and pliable, like Sofia's usual type. "*Ciao, bella.* You have fun with your model, no?"

"No," Ariel muttered, returning Sofia's kiss-on-each-cheek and hoping she could complete this life portrait in record time.

Having fun with the model should be the furthest thing from her mind.

Chapter Six

Cooper stood outside the gallery, admiring the wide windows, cream rendered walls, and green fretwork. He'd checked out this site many times over the last few months, even though his dad had been handling the acquisition, and each time Cooper had been more intent on assessing the gallery's street position and how the space could be developed than aesthetics.

Colour by Dreams.

Nice name. A name depicting hope and imagination and creativity.

Shame he had to tear it all down.

He'd never had qualms in the business arena before, no point starting now, even if the gallery's owner had piqued his interest.

He pushed through the front door, dodging the ridiculous wind chimes signalling his entry, and hoped Ariel was in a receptive mood. He had to tell her the truth before this farce went any further. Lying didn't sit well with him and he'd always been scrupulously honest in past deals.

Though where had that got him? Bound to his father

with the same ironclad contract all Vance employees signed, trying to be the best he could and now chaffing to escape the tyrant's clutches.

"Hi, you're right on time." Ariel strolled into the gallery from the back studio, having little trouble with the silly beads dividing the rooms, and he faltered, staggered by the power of her smile and the cheeky glint in her sparkling eyes.

Tonight, she wore a white ruffled shirt, a plum crushed velvet vest, black pleated shorts, and pink wedges that made her legs look impossibly long. A crazy ensemble that would've appeared ridiculous on any other woman but on Ariel it looked like haute couture. She wore her clothes with aplomb, and he smiled, thinking an eye patch wouldn't have looked out of place with her rakish pirate outfit.

"Something funny?"

"No, just admiring what you're wearing."

She blushed, the hint of pink accentuating the green of her eyes and the rich gold of her hair, which she wore in a high ponytail.

With her straightforward manner and sassy mouth, he didn't think she'd be prone to blushing.

"You like my taste in clothes?" Her eyebrows arched. "I find that hard to believe. Anyway, enough of the chit-chat. Let's get started."

Hell. This was going to be harder than he thought.

He cleared his throat. "Actually, that's what I want to talk to you about."

"Give me a break." She rolled her eyes, perched on a stool behind the counter, and rested her chin in her hands. "Don't you think we moved past the whole virginal act last night?"

Cooper stared at her, torn between wanting to laugh out

loud and call her bluff. Every time he tried to tell her the truth, she either interrupted him or shot him down with some smart-ass remark.

He'd give it one more shot. If she wouldn't listen, he'd shelve his good intentions and use tonight as one last opportunity to get some inside info on the opposition before approaching her with his plans for the gallery.

And when the time came, he wouldn't take no for an answer, no matter how cute the word sounded coming out of her sweet mouth.

"I think you should know more about me, listen to what I have to say, then—"

"Nope. Sorry. No can do." She stood quickly, her ponytail bouncing like a jaunty flag amidships. "Please don't take this the wrong way, but I'm not interested in getting to know you. I'm not interested in you period. You're here in a work capacity and that's it. You sit, I paint. End of story."

She flounced past him, the same weird, intoxicating scent of jasmine and oranges as enticing as the rest of her wafting over him, and locked the front door.

End of story, huh?

Fine.

If Miss Bossy-Boots wouldn't give him a chance to explain, he'd take what he could from tonight and try the professional approach in the morning.

"On the contrary, this story is just beginning," he murmured, following her into the studio with an extra spring to his step.

Chapter Seven

The man was a menace.

The harder Ariel tried to concentrate on sketching, the more Cooper would smile, smirk, or chat.

She could strangle him with her bare hands.

Though she didn't want to get that close, considering he wasn't wearing any clothes—bar the requisite boxers, which she'd insisted he keep on again.

Chicken.

"Tell me more about this painting. Where's it going to hang?"

She silently cursed as her charcoal slewed. He'd spoken just as she'd captured the curve of his hip—and butt—but she didn't want to dwell on that piece of anatomy. Time enough when she'd have to study it, without the cover of navy cotton boxers.

"This is a private commission, a gift for a friend's sister, so it will hang in her home."

"This isn't the fabled friend-of-a-friend and it's actually for your private collection?"

His smug chuckle made Ariel grit her teeth, as she wondered if the use of duct tape over a model's mouth would be frowned upon by any worker's union.

"Sorry to disappoint, but this sort of art doesn't do it for me." *Liar.*

"Then what does?"

Damn it, she'd been the queen of quick comebacks all her life. She had to be, living on the streets. But this guy fired back with a skill to be envied.

"None of your business, Mr. Shy-and-Retiring, before whipping off your clothes in record time."

He pretended to pout. "Hey, that's not fair. You practically shoved me behind that screen, and I was absolutely terrified you'd actually rip them off me if I didn't hurry up."

His cocky smile showed her just how *terrified* he'd been at the thought of her tearing off his clothes, while simultaneously doing crazy things to her insides: her stomach flipped and somersaulted, a reminder she hadn't eaten dinner. She'd tried before Cooper arrived, but the thought of seeing all that gorgeous expanse of bare, tanned skin again had ruined her appetite.

"You wish," she said, aiming for a frown but failing miserably when their gazes locked over her easel and something zinged between them, a zap of invisible electricity that made her heart join her stomach in the gymnastic stakes. "Don't you ever shut up?"

Ariel's retort sounded short and sharp in the loaded silence, and she ducked behind the easel, buying valuable time to gather her wits and get her breathing under control. Alongside her pounding heart, her lungs had joined the party and deprived her of much-needed oxygen.

Must be more of those nasty paint fumes affecting her again.

Yeah, right.

"It's pretty boring sitting here doing nothing but pose for you," he said. "A little conversation breaks the monotony."

He sounded reasonable enough and she snuck a peek, wondering if he was being serious or teasing her again. To her mortification, he caught her furtive glance and winked, exacerbating her embarrassment.

Yeah, she could definitely strangle him.

Once she'd captured his exquisite body on canvas, that is.

"Have you always been an artist?"

She picked up a charcoal nub, determined to ignore him, but his question seemed innocuous enough and his voice had lost its teasing lilt.

"I loved drawing as a kid. I graduated from chalk drawings on sidewalks to etchings on paper. When other kids were playing hopscotch, I'd be sketching their faces. Later, I did a bachelor of arts to help with the teaching side of things if I ever chose to go down that path, but basically, I've worked alongside Barb here forever. We loved art so much…"

Her fingers stilled as she wondered what had possessed her to reveal so much to a guy she didn't know, a guy she didn't even particularly like that much.

The cosy ambience of the studio at night seemed conducive to shared confidences, but Cooper wasn't a friend and she'd be smarter remembering it.

"Anyway, that's it for now. I think I've done all I'm going to do tonight. It's been a long day." She didn't look at him as she wiped her hands on a dusty rag, wishing he'd hurry up and get dressed so she could shove him out the door.

For a guy she hardly knew—and didn't want to know—Cooper had her in a spin, answering questions she'd usually ignore, deriving comfort from confiding in another human when she had so little social contact with anyone.

What a sad case.

"Ariel?"

"Yeah?"

She looked up, grateful he'd slipped into jeans and a white T shirt quickly, sensing her need to get rid of him without delay.

"Whatever happens, you should be proud of what you've done with this place."

"Thanks," she said, surprised by his serious expression and somewhat confused by what he'd said.

But she was too tired to think about it let alone ask him to explain as she hurried him to the door, flicking the lock and all but wrenching it off its hinges in her haste to see the back of him.

As the door swung open and a chilly gust of wind blew it out of her hands, Chelsea Lynch, her protégée, rushed into the gallery in a flurry of turquoise denim, red pashmina, emerald scarf, and floppy fuchsia beanie.

Cooper took a polite step back, nodded at Chelsea, and turned to Ariel. "I'll see you tomorrow. We really need to talk."

Ariel flashed him a tight smile, thinking her talking days with the too good-looking model were over if she had to finish his portrait with her sanity intact.

Chelsea's head swung between the two of them, her eyes wide with shock, her mouth hanging open before pointing an accusing finger at Cooper and shouting, "What's he doing here?"

"Cooper's a model."

"Like hell he is."

Chelsea unwound her scarf in furious swirls, not taking her flashing hazel eyes off Cooper for a second. "He's the scumbag who's been buying up the street and I bet he has his sights set on this place next."

Ariel's protest died on her lips as she saw Cooper's stricken, guilty expression a second before she acted on instinct, her palm landing squarely in the middle of his broad chest and shoving him out the door.

Hard.

Chapter Eight

Ariel tried to slam the door in Cooper's face but took a moment too long. The lying cretin stuck one of his shoes in the doorjamb and as tempted as she was to amputate it, she couldn't afford a lawsuit on top of everything else at the minute.

"Get out!" Ariel jiggled the door, hoping he'd take the hint with the way she'd shoved him out the door.

"Let me explain—"

"Explain what? That you're a miserable, lying snake or that you're so desperate you'd take off your clothes to get inside info for your proposed takeover?"

She planted her hands on her hips, fury surging through her body at being taken for a fool. Living on the streets as a youngster, people had assumed she was stupid, equating a dowdy appearance with nil intelligence, and she'd hated it.

She'd shown everyone and then some.

Exactly how she would show Cooper whatever-his-name-was after giving him a verbal flaying he'd never forget.

"He took his clothes off?" Chelsea's eyes bulged as she

plucked off her beanie and ran a hand through her short, spiky, red hair. "That *is* desperate."

"It wasn't like that," Cooper said, a faint pink flushing his tanned cheeks as his bashful gaze focussed on hers. "I tried to tell you the truth a few times but you always shot me down, talked over me, or didn't want to know."

Ariel rolled her eyes. "Give me a break. Guys like you can talk underwater with a mouth full of marbles for business, and you think you couldn't get the message across because I wouldn't let you?" She snorted. "What a load of crap. You kept your big mouth shut because you wanted to sleaze your way into my good graces."

"That's telling him," Chelsea murmured, and Ariel shot her a quelling glance to keep out of it.

While Ariel was grateful for her star pupil outing the rat, she could fight her own battles. Always had, always would.

"Can we talk in private?" Cooper's steady gaze locked on hers, urgent, compelling, willing her to listen.

Too bad for him, she'd listened to enough of his lies already.

She shook her head. "I'm not interested in anything you have to say. Now, if you don't mind removing your big foot from my door and shoving it back into your mouth, I have work to do."

"This isn't the end," Cooper said, his earnest expression meaning business as he removed his foot from the doorway.

"That's what you think."

Ariel slammed the door, grateful for the double reinforced glass. It saved her from shattering the windows and afforded a fantastic view of the look on Cooper's face.

If she didn't know any better, she'd say he appeared ashamed.

But that couldn't be right. Guys like him didn't have a conscience and they never took no for an answer. They wheeled and dealed their way to the top regardless of the little people trampled in the process.

Well, she had news for him. This little person wouldn't let him near her place again let alone allow him to buy it and ruin her plans for the future.

Cooper the marauding model could develop some other property to acquire, preferably in Timbuktu.

"That was awesome," Chelsea said, slapping her on the back. "You sure showed him who was boss."

Fatigued, Ariel watched Cooper march up the street past the organic fruiterers, the vegan takeout stand, and the Nepalese homewares, before turning the corner where he'd probably hidden some fancy sports car.

Lying jerk.

Damn lying jerk that had gotten under her skin in two short meetings. And to make matters worse, she had to work from memory to finish the portrait when the last thing she felt like doing was resurrecting memories of the jerk's body and how great it would look on canvas.

"You okay?" Chelsea asked.

"Yeah. How did you know who he was?"

"I've seen him around the Fitzroy area over the last few months. Mr Fancy-Schmancy works for a company that is responsible for ousting the Ng's from the corner grocer's, the Bortelli's from their café, and closing down the old Irish pub, all in the name of *development*." Chelsea held up her index fingers on both hands and made inverted comma signs. "I hate guys like him. They've never done it tough. They don't know the first thing about the area or locals like me who live in it. They bulldoze their way in and rip lives apart. Tell me you won't let them get the gallery."

THE CHARMER

"Not if I have any say in it," Ariel muttered, knowing she'd be in for the fight of her life if Cooper set his sights on her gallery.

Chelsea threw her arms wide and did a three-sixty. "I love this place. All the local kids do. Barb made it more welcoming than any halfway house and you've continued the tradition. You can't let those bloodsuckers take it."

Ariel managed a weary smile, buoyed by Chelsea's enthusiasm but more afraid than she'd ever been. She'd known about the property developers buying up every last piece of prime Brunswick Street land, but to hear Chelsea verbalise it somehow made the threat all the more real.

"Don't worry. I have no intention of letting them anywhere near *Colour by Dreams*."

Chelsea clapped her hands like an excited child. "Good, because my first showing is here in a week and I want the world to see my brilliance."

"And your modesty," Ariel said with a wry grin, trying to banish the threatening image of Cooper's final glower before he marched away out of her mind and what it could mean for the gallery. "Now, how about some tea and you can tell me why you dropped by?"

Chelsea lead the way out the back, bouncing with vitality, her pashmina trailing in her wake like a bright flag. Ariel followed, knowing it would take more than herbal tea to dispel her anxiety at the moment.

"Wow!"

The minute Chelsea laid eyes on the preliminary portrait sketches Ariel had done of Cooper, her red suede boots flew across the floor to stop dead in front of the easel.

"I'll take that as a compliment to my artistic skills and not the subject in question," Ariel said, busying herself making tea and hoping she had enough sketches to create a final portrait from.

Chelsea grinned, tearing her gaze from the sketches for a second. "Don't get me wrong, I think you're the best artist this side of the Louvre, but wowee. That guy might be a slime-ball but he is one hot slime-ball."

"I should've known he was too good to be true," Ariel said, trying not to scald herself as she poured boiling water into mugs, her hands shaking in anger at how Cooper had fooled her. "Model, my butt."

"Unfortunately, doesn't look like you got to that part, worse luck."

Chelsea winked as Ariel handed her a mug of steaming lemongrass and ginger, the young woman's favourite, while she tentatively sipped at her peppermint brew, the steam heating her cheeks.

Or was that the thought of Cooper's butt? The same butt she should've kicked given half a chance.

"Shouldn't be a problem. I can improvise." Sadly, Ariel knew her imagination wasn't *that* good.

"Whatever."

Chelsea shrugged and took a seat on one of the ruby sofas, curling her long, legging-clad legs beneath her while she cradled her mug.

"What's with the long face?"

Ariel didn't need any more problems right now. She had enough of her own to keep her busy into the next century.

"Do you really think I'm any good at all this art stuff?" Chelsea's large hazel eyes radiated doubt and Ariel smiled, confident she could solve this problem easily.

Taking a seat next to the nineteen-year-old, she said, "Do you trust my judgement?"

"Yeah."

"And you know how tough it is to get a showing in a gallery in Melbourne?"

The corners of Chelsea's mouth turned upward. "Yeah."

"Plus you know how busy I am, right?"

Chelsea grinned and sat up straighter. "Right."

"You're a smart girl. Do you think I would waste my time if I didn't think you're talented and inspired and are going to be the next big thing?"

"When you put it that way..." Chelsea plucked Ariel's mug out of her hand, deposited it next to hers on the floor, and flung her arms around her. "You're the best. Barb was so lucky to have someone like you take over from her."

"I'm the lucky one," Ariel murmured, blinking back sudden tears.

If only she could keep the likes of Cooper from taking away the only place she'd ever known as home, she'd be very lucky indeed.

Chapter Nine

"Where are we at with acquiring that gallery?"

Cooper refrained from glaring at his father, especially with a conference table full of developers, wishing his dad didn't keep pushing so hard. He said he'd handle it.

Yeah, like you handled it last night?

Silently cursing, he shuffled the papers in front of him and faced the curious looks of the men who'd invested millions in the project so far. He'd give them what they wanted to hear before settling the deal one way or another.

"As you all know, Ariel Wallace isn't keen on selling. However, I've met with her the last two days and I'm optimistic she'll change her mind."

She had to. He needed to escape this company and his father's overbearing presence, like yesterday.

"What makes you think you'll succeed where I didn't?"

This time, Cooper couldn't stop his swift glare of condemnation at his dad. Eric had taken professional jealousy to extremes in the past, but did he have to air his feelings in this forum?

Quelling his anger, Cooper addressed the table at large. "Eric, everyone here knows you're a top negotiator, but I've established a rapport with Miss Wallace."

Yeah, they'd grown real close if her shoving him out the door constituted camaraderie. "I'm confident that with a few more meetings, she'll come to the party."

His farewell party, that is.

The day she signed on the dotted line is the day he would be free. Free of his contract, free of *Vance Corp*, free of seeing the cold calculating edge in his father's eyes every time he walked into the room.

"Good." Eric barely inclined his head in Cooper's direction before continuing. "I've sealed the deal on several properties around the block from the gallery and we need that piece of land ASAP."

Eric tapped at a key on his computer and a giant screen lit up with a presentation behind him. "These are the preliminary plans, but once we secure the gallery, we can demolish it, along with the old houses behind, and create a six storey apartment block. With property prices continuing to increase in suburbs surrounding the CBD, that's a killing for all of us."

Eric stared at Cooper with contempt, as if saying, 'and you want to leave all this behind? You think you can match me? Beat me at my own game?'

"Any questions?"

Cooper met his father's gaze directly, knowing now wasn't the time or place to ask 'why did you change? Why the competitive jealousy? Will I ever make you proud?'

Instead, he settled for keeping the peace just like he had every day for the last eleven months since he'd graduated and signed on the dotted line with dear old Dad. Back then, he'd been full of ideals, full of enthusiasm, and his father's lousy attitude had whittled it away to this: some stupid deal so he could back out of his legally binding contract.

"The plans look good," Cooper said, his tone well-modulated despite the anger coursing through him courtesy of his father belittling him as usual. "I'm just as eager to get this deal done as all of you, so perhaps we can reconvene next week?"

That should give him enough time to talk sense into the bohemian harridan who'd tossed him out of her gallery like yesterday's garbage. He'd make sure of it.

"Fine. Meeting adjourned." Eric headed straight for the built-in bar in the corner of the conference room and Cooper knew he'd swap shop talk with his cronies over a bourbon or two, boasting about his latest acquisitions and his plans for the future.

Schmoozing wasn't for Cooper. He had more important things to do with his time, like getting Ariel to listen to his pitch.

He assumed she wouldn't open her door to him again let alone hear what he had to say, but he planned to change all that.

Starting now.

Chapter Ten

"You despicable low-life."

Ariel slashed at the canvas with her brush, streaking across the blank expanse while glaring daggers at the sketch of Cooper propped next to it.

She'd been trying to capture his likeness on canvas all morning and had tense shoulders, a tight neck, and three ruined canvases—all recycled, thank goodness—for her trouble.

Her muse had deserted her.

Unfortunately, she had a sneaking suspicion her muse had hitched a ride on the despicable low-life's broad shoulders and cruised straight out the door.

She'd tried everything: burning her favourite lime and tangerine candles, dabbing neroli—her favourite scent—on her pulse points for inspiration and to calm her mind, wearing her lucky holly garland on her head, and a five minute meditation that usually worked wonders if her imagination clogged.

The result? Nothing helped. And to make matters worse, Sofia had called, gushing about some fancy charity event at her sister's place where everyone who was anyone would see the portrait and inundate Ariel with work—she wished—and imploring her to finish it a week early.

Which gave her exactly six days to get the portrait finished.

It would've been a cinch if she had a normal model and not some delusional businessman happy to whip off his clothes to get what he wanted.

Staring at the sketches of Cooper, she could've happily drawn devil's horns and pointy fangs on his smug face, but they were all she had...and that wasn't much.

Sighing, she closed her eyes, trying to conjure up the memory of his form, hoping to translate it to canvas. Deep blue eyes, too long dark hair, strong jaw, broad chest, great pecs, tapered waist, long legs...

To her annoyance, she recalled images of Cooper's amazing body too readily. Excellent for finishing the portrait; disastrous for her peace of mind.

The wind chimes over the front door tinkled and her eyes opened.

"Can I help you..." she trailed off as the object of her vivid recollection a second ago strutted into the gallery, the epitome of the slick businessman she now knew him to be: fancy suit, white shirt, duck-egg blue tie that matched his striking eyes. He looked amazing but she preferred him in jeans and T-shirt.

Are you insane?

She didn't prefer him at all. Or was that in nothing at all?

"Go away," she said, planting both hands on the counter and glaring at him with as much disdain she could muster.

"No can do."

He stopped on the opposite side of the counter and

Ariel wished it was wider. He was too close, too masculine, too everything.

"I have a proposal for you."

"After two nights? Wow, you must be really desperate to get your grubby hands on this place, but sorry, I wouldn't marry you if you gargled a litre of turpentine and painted the street red."

He grinned, a cocky smile that screamed 'bring it on.' "I'm not here with a marriage proposal. You strike me as a smart woman and in the interests of your business I thought you should hear me out."

"You thought wrong," she blurted, not ready to hear anything he had to say.

She was too angry with him: angry he'd lied, angry he'd ruined a project so vital to the viability of the gallery, but most of all, angry with herself for the slight, inane leap of joy she'd experienced when he'd come back.

He ignored her petulant outburst. "This will only take five minutes of your time. Believe me, it's important."

She wouldn't believe him if he was the last man on earth, but something about his steady gaze and open expression had her shrugging her shoulders and leading him out the back.

"Five minutes," she said, propping on her ergonomic stool, not caring if he stood or sat. He wouldn't be around that long if she had any say in the matter.

Chapter Eleven

"What's that on your head?"

Not exactly what Cooper had in mind as a stunning opening to his pitch but he couldn't talk sense to a woman wearing a Christmas wreath on her head, even if she wore it with the aplomb of a queen sporting a priceless tiara.

Ariel frowned and patted her head, the frown disappearing when she touched the weird crown. "This is my lucky garland. I often paint in it."

"It looks like a Christmas tree gone wrong."

Rather than taking it off in embarrassment as he expected, she adjusted the angle until it sat like a cheeky halo perched at odds with her crazy curls.

"I made it years ago during my first Christmas with Aunt Barb."

The smirk that had been playing around her mouth vanished and Cooper wished he hadn't seen the vulnerability behind her eyes.

He was here on business, to present a clear plan to benefit them both. He didn't want to hear about this woman

THE CHARMER

Barb who Ariel held in such high esteem or feel the slightest twinge of guilt that in following his dreams he'd probably have to tear hers down.

She was young. She'd get over it. She could take the money, and start a new gallery somewhere else.

"Your five minutes started about thirty-seconds ago so whatever you have to say, make it snappy." Ariel's expression hardened, her green eyes flinty, her mouth compressed in a thin line.

Squaring his shoulders, confident a softer approach would work rather than railroading her like he usually did with the rest of his clients, Cooper met her cool gaze head on.

"Firstly, I'd like to apologise for not telling you the truth earlier. You were right, I had plenty of opportunity and could've let you in on my identity sooner."

"Why didn't you?"

"Honestly? You intrigued me. I had my spiel all worked out when I first walked in here but before I knew what was happening, you'd bustled me out the back and told me to take off my clothes. I guess the Neanderthal in me took over and I kind of liked it." He shrugged, feeling like an idiot for admitting the truth but hoping she valued his honesty. "Stupid, I know, but the whole situation was extraordinary and once we started talking, I couldn't leave."

By her dubious expression, his honesty hadn't worked.

Her eyes narrowed as she pinned him with an assessing stare. "I think you didn't want to leave because you thought you could weasel inside info out of me before honing in for the kill."

"That too." He winced at her brutal but accurate assessment. "Pretty despicable, but I was going to tell you the truth even if that girl hadn't outed me. You probably won't believe this but the whole thing was a bit of an ego trip—"

"That I believe." She rolled her eyes before tapping her watch. "Three minutes left."

He held up his hands like he had nothing to hide. "Okay, my idea is this. I have a business proposal to present to you. It will probably take a few hours all up to do it justice and I was hoping you'd give me the time."

"No."

Short and sharp, without the slightest hint of thawing, and he pushed on, hoping she understood how things worked in the business world and wouldn't be offended by his next offer.

"I'll pay you for your time."

"What?"

If her eyebrows shot any higher, they'd tangle in that crazy wreath perched on her wayward curls.

"In the world I come from, everyone charges by the hour, from lawyers to architects. I see your time as being no different and I'm willing to compensate you for the few hours it takes to deliver my pitch."

"You're willing to compensate me...how *generous*."

If her strange, high-pitched fake voice and the clenched hands twisting the cuffs of her crushed velvet shorts weren't a dead giveaway of what she thought of his offer, her sarcasm clued him in.

"The point I'm trying to make is, this place is your business, so your time is just as valuable as everyone else's and I want to recognise that."

Better, much better, and by the softening of her ramrod straight posture, she thought so too.

"I don't want your money."

"But you'll still listen to my pitch?"

THE CHARMER

He held his breath, wishing this bohemian beauty didn't hold his future in the palm of her paint-stained hand. She had to listen to his pitch and she had to go for it. He couldn't contemplate any other outcome.

Forging ahead with plans for his own company after a lengthy legal battle to escape the contract would drive an irreversible wedge between him and his father, when he was hoping some much needed time apart might actually make his dad's heart grow fonder.

Yeah, and Santa would be asking him to renovate and develop the North Pole any day now.

But he had to try. He loved his dad too much to give up on him.

To Cooper's surprise, Ariel's face cleared. Her brow smoothed, her lips tilted up at the corners, and her green eyes sparkled with excitement.

Uh-oh. This couldn't be good.

He'd seen that same look when she'd all but pushed him into her studio the first night and told him to get his gear off.

"I won't accept your money but how about we do a fair trade for time?"

"Sounds feasible," he said, not liking her smug smirk.

He liked the tense, uncertain Ariel a lot more than her cheeky counterpart who made him want to drop his business ideals at the door and get creative with this sprite-like woman in a variety of imaginative ways.

"What did you have in mind?"

To his surprise, Ariel slid off her stool and walked around the counter between them to place a finger under his chin and tilt his head this way and that. Before he could compute her touching him, she lowered her hand and stepped back, continuing to study him like a prized masterpiece.

"This is perfect." She clapped her hands and smiled at him, the type of mega smile that could melt a guy's hardened heart if he wasn't careful. "You pose for me until I finish the portrait and I'll listen to your boring proposal. How's that for fair trade? A few hours modelling for a few hours of hearing you ramble about a business proposition I have zero interest in?"

Cooper stared at her, unwillingly admiring her glowing eyes, her wide confident smile. He bit back his first gut response of 'no way,' knowing that a smart businessman would take every opportunity that came his way and turn it into something big.

In this case, it may be the only chance he got. She'd let him in the door, she'd heard him out, and she'd agreed to listen to his plans for this place.

Posing almost naked, albeit on a hard stool for a few hours, would be nothing if he pulled this deal off.

"You've got a deal."

He held out his hand, managing a genuine smile when she placed her tiny hand in his despite the jolt physical contact brought. By the slight widening of her eyes, she felt it too but pulled away before he could analyse it further.

Not that he wanted to. She wasn't his type. He preferred cool, aloof women who were happy with the occasional date and had no expectations.

A warm, vibrant, creative woman like Ariel would be nothing but trouble for a level-headed guy like him and he'd make sure he concentrated on business around her.

He didn't have room in his life for anything else.

Chapter Twelve

Twisting Cooper's proposal to suit her ends had come to Ariel in a flash of brilliance and the way she saw it, she'd come out on top. She'd get to finish the portrait and collect the much needed money for it, and in exchange, she'd spend a few boring hours listening to him prattle on about his plans for her gallery, plans that would never see the light of day when she refused him.

Easy.

"I'd love a coffee," he said, dwarfing everything in the tiny kitchenette of her studio.

"Herbal tea is better for you," Ariel said.

"I'll stick with coffee, thanks."

"Suit yourself," she said, bustling around the kitchen and prepping their drinks before handing him a steaming mug of decaf he'd requested, knowing he'd find it lacking. He looked like a double espresso hold-the-milk-and-sugar type of guy to her. "Speaking of which, you're looking a lot more uptight in that suit than the other night. What were you trying to do then, con the crazy artist in your slumming clothes?"

His mouth twitched. "I happen to live in jeans and T-shirts outside the office."

"And?"

"And I thought you wouldn't be as intimidated if I turned up dressed casual."

Ariel grinned. The guy was sneaky. And sexy, way too sexy.

"You better be careful, Mr.Big Shot. That's the second time in half an hour you've sounded honest. Didn't think your type had it in you."

"If you're trying to bait me, forget it. I've got a thick skin." His laconic grin did crazy things to her pulse. "Comes with taking off my clothes for perverted women posing as artists."

So he had a sense of humour. She refused to be charmed. Besides, he'd need to see the funny side when she knocked his business proposal for the gallery on its head.

"The human body is a work of art," she said. "I can't help it if your head is filled with taking over buildings and ruining people's lives rather than appreciating the finer things in life like I do."

She kept her tone light, enjoying trading banter with someone who could match her even though her quip held a barb of truth. She would never understand how he could barge into businesses and turn them upside down with scant regard for the little people. Sure, he probably justified his actions with money, but that's all a successful guy like him understood.

"Have you ever considered I improve people's lives rather than ruin them?" He took a sip of coffee and grimaced, hiding his distaste behind a discreet cough.

"Whatever lets you sleep at night."

THE CHARMER

She drained her cup of peppermint tea and peered into the bottom, a silly old habit considering she'd switched to bags and didn't use loose leaves any more. Too bad, considering she could use a bit of forecasting right now: like how the portrait would turn out, would she keep the gallery, would she be able to keep her interest in the model purely professional.

"Would you like a refill before we get down to business and establish a few ground rules?"

"No thanks."

He beat a hasty path to the sink where he rinsed his mug in record time as Ariel followed, chuckling softly. He thought she'd assume he was being super helpful but she knew better; she'd seen his three-quarters full mug and what better way to surreptitiously tip the whole lot down the sink than pretend to wash? As suspected, he wasn't a decaf guy.

"What's this about ground rules?"

She waited until he moved away from the sink before rinsing her mug. She'd jokingly called him a big shot but Cooper was just that, big in every way. It was more than a size thing though, something about his supreme confidence, his imposing aura, the way he carried himself.

Usually, guys like him intimidated her but Cooper had an innate kindness she sensed, an indefinable quality that drew him to her even if she kicked and screamed all the way.

Drying her hands on a tea towel, she resisted the urge to flick it at his butt as he turned away and walked out of the kitchenette. Jeez, what was it about this guy that brought out her impish side?

The funny thing was, now they'd established where things were going and she'd get her way with the portrait, she couldn't stop teasing him and trying to get him to loosen up.

"Would you like to take a seat and we can discuss this?"

He shook his head and glanced at his watch. "Can we make this snappy? I've already been here longer than anticipated."

So much for teasing and lightening up.

"Fine. I just wanted to make sure we both understand the time involved in our trade. I probably need you to sit for another four sessions, about an hour each. How long will your pitch take?"

"Around two, but that's fine. When I make a deal, I stick to it."

He folded his arms, the fingers on his right hand drumming against his left bicep. If he started tapping his feet, whistling and staring at the ceiling in impatience, she wouldn't have been surprised. The guy switched from light banter to cold indifference in a flash. The decaf must've really irked.

"Good. As for the posing part, you know it's a life portrait?" She couldn't resist pushing his buttons.

"So you've told me." He didn't smile or smirk but a faint pink stained his tanned cheeks.

"Just to put your mind at ease, you won't have to get completely naked. What you've been doing so far is great, with your leg covering uh..." Great, now it was her turn to blush. "Anyway, I just have to do the bottom half, then get some detailed sketches of your hands, feet, and face, and transfer the lot onto canvas. Once I've finished, I'll hear your pitch."

And see the back of you, literally. "You okay with all that?"

"Fine. Can we get started tonight?"

THE CHARMER

He hadn't lost his antsy look. If anything, it had intensified. Boy, he must really want her to hear his proposal.

"See you back here at seven."

"Good. See you then."

With a mock half salute, he all but ran out of the studio, through the gallery, and towards the front door.

"Cooper, I forgot something."

He paused with his hand on the door knob. "What's that?"

"Bring a small fig leaf. It might come in handy for camouflage."

She tried to keep a straight face and couldn't, her laughter following him out the door as his exasperated expression told her exactly what he thought of her sense of humour.

Chapter Thirteen

"Can I take a look?"

Cooper wiggled his fingers and toes in an effort to restore circulation to his extremities, grateful this modelling gig would be over soon.

Not that he didn't enjoy spending one on one time with Ariel, who surprised him at every turn, but he needed to seal the deal before next Friday. He had a feeling the investors wouldn't be too impressed if he stalled again.

As for his dad, he'd been close to up and leaving, contract or not, several times this week. They didn't just not see eye to eye any more, they seemed to be on a different path altogether. Eric had stringent ideas regarding his company's future and he treated Cooper like a subordinate whose ideas were crap. He'd had enough.

"Stop moving. I need to capture the arch of your right foot tonight and I'm done." She glared at him over the easel, dabbing her brush in the paints on a worn palette next to her before returning her attention to the canvas.

Even with a smudge of paint on her cheek, her curls escaping their customary bandanna—zebra stripes tonight—

and falling across her forehead, and dark circles under her eyes courtesy of how hard she must be pushing to finish this portrait in record time, she was the most beautiful woman he'd ever seen.

From the bottom of her pink raffia ballet shoes to her anglaise bolero worn over a chartreuse ribbed singlet, she looked adorable, a bright spark in his otherwise dull day.

As for those shorts she wore...for the last three nights, tonight included, he'd been subjected to long, gorgeous legs poking out from truly ugly shorts. Vintage tartan checks, awful blue flowers against mustard backgrounds, and purple polka dots against turquoise. Thankfully, her eclectic taste in clothes hadn't blinded him to the beauty of her luscious legs and he'd done his fair share of looking while she'd been studying him.

"When you say you're done, is that done as in finished completely?"

"You wish," she said, absentmindedly twisting a curl around a finger while dabbing at the canvas.

Actually, he didn't. The logic, business side of his brain was yelling 'hell yeah' but his lonely side, the emotional side he'd deliberately shut down courtesy of his father's increasing indifference, wished they could stay ensconced in her cosy studio forever.

"How much longer?"

Exhaling loudly, she stabbed her brush into a glass jar of water, rolled her neck a few times, stood, and arched her back in a stretch. "Anyone ever tell you that you talk too much?"

"Anyone ever tell you that you're great at avoiding answering questions?"

After another cat-like stretch that had him averting his eyes in record time when she looked at him, she said, "If you must know, I'm almost done. I just need to get a few details of your face completed and that's it."

"Tonight?"

His heart sank. As much as he liked being here, he'd had a long day at the office and needed to finalise a report for a presentation first thing Monday morning.

She laughed, a genuine throaty chuckle that made him want to join in. "With you sounding so enthusiastic, I guess not. Why don't you get dressed and I'll make us a hot drink."

Cooper tried not to screw up his face. If he had to endure one more cup of her foul-tasting herbal brews or equally horrid coffee, he'd happily walk away from this deal here and now.

"I've got a better idea. Why don't we grab a coffee at the café across the street? The place looks new, they could probably do with the business."

"Before you tear it down, you mean?"

Her smile vanished and he couldn't tell if she was serious or joking. Either way, he was too tired to argue.

"Whatever you decide to do, I'm heading over there for the largest strong black they've got. I have a long night ahead of me."

A flicker of remorse crossed her face and she disguised it by tidying up her work space. "Hot date, huh?"

"Yeah, the hottest," he said, sliding his oldest cotton T-shirt over his head and slipping into faded denim. "Just my slinky little lap top and me."

"Do you enjoy what you do?"

He stepped out from behind the screen to find her perched on the stool he'd just vacated, those spectacular legs tucked up on the rung underneath, a curious look on her paint-smudged face.

THE CHARMER

"It's challenging. I like seeing things develop and take shape from the infant stages right through to the finished product. You can identify with that, surely?"

He expected a vehement rebuttal but to his surprise she nodded, a tiny frown between her brows as if she was pondering what he'd said.

"Yeah, I can. Apart from the whole creative side of art, I love seeing something develop before my eyes. It's hard work but the reward is worth it."

"Exactly."

They locked stares, his challenging, hers curious. However, before she could chastise him for being a developer or tease him about his uptight ways, he turned away and shrugged into his leather jacket.

"Right, I have a mega strong espresso waiting with my name all over it. I'm out of here."

He sent her a casual wave, a major part of him wishing she'd join him. They'd chatted a fair bit while she worked but he still didn't know what made her tick. She'd deliberately kept things light between them and he hadn't pushed, despite hoping to understand the rationale behind her absolute refusal to sell the gallery.

There had to be more to it, more than a promise to a dead aunt.

He'd bide his time, knowing the pitch he'd prepared to deliver would convince her. If there was one thing he had learned, the gorgeous woman with the kooky dress sense had a brain in her head and hopefully, she'd see his proposal for what it was: a smart business decision and a win-win solution for them all.

He'd barely taken a step when she slid off the stool, picked up a giant straw hold-all that looked like it could easily contain the proverbial sink and then some, and smoothed her wrinkled shorts.

"I think I'll come with you. I've been cooped up in this place working every night for a week straight. A change of scene will do me good."

"So it's not my scintillating company that enticed you to join me?"

"Honestly? No."

She matched his sardonic grin, tilting her chin up to meet his gaze head-on. The minute he reached out to touch her cheek, he knew it was a mistake. But then, he'd hardly been his usual rational, conventional self since setting foot in this place.

"You have a paint smudge right here." He slid his finger down her cheek, slowly, gently, her velvety smooth skin a magnet to his touch.

He should've pulled away the second her luminous green eyes widened and her lush mouth formed a small O, but instead he lingered, savouring the close contact, the intimacy enveloping them as surely as the heady perfume she wore.

"Thanks," she said, stepping away to rub at her cheek, her eyes never leaving his. "Just give me a second to get cleaned up and I'll be right with you."

"No problems."

He lied.

His reaction to the beautiful artist was definitely a problem, a major one.

He had no qualms about her focussing on the business side of the deal he proposed but the million dollar question was, could he?

Chapter Fourteen

Ariel snuggled into the comfy armchair, loving the homely ambience of The Cypress Tree. The new owners had done wonders with the place and she wasn't surprised to see it packed on a Friday night.

"What'll you have?"

"I'll have a decaf skinny soy turmeric latte, please."

Cooper stared at her in disbelief. "You're kidding, right? Tell me that's not a real drink."

Ariel chuckled. "To a boring, strong black, caffeine-swilling coffee hick like you, I guess not."

Shaking his head, Cooper placed their order with a waitress sporting a magenta Mohawk and enough facial piercings to keep the local silversmiths in business for the next decade. Though the punk hairstyle didn't do much for her, Ariel admired the teenager's gold lame hot-pants and wanted to ask her which boutique she frequented.

"At the risk of sounding like the hick you just accused me of, is it fancy dress night at this place?"

Ariel grinned, knowing exactly what he meant, but wanting to tease him a little. "Why would you say that?"

Cooper's gaze traversed the cosy café, his eyes growing wider by the minute. "For starters, there's a guy over there wearing cow-print leather pants and a red vest with nothing underneath. Then there's another guy wearing orange leather chaps over denim shorts. Throw in the overabundance of black spandex, gold sequins, and silver metallic objects protruding from every body part imaginable, do you blame me for asking?"

Ariel shrugged, saddened by the huge gulf between them. They really were from opposite ends of the planet in every way: their tastes, their occupations, their thinking.

Yet she still found him attractive. Go figure?

Damn hormones.

"I don't blame you for asking. I'm not surprised a big shot like you wouldn't know about a cultural hub like Brunswick Street. Take another look around."

She swept her hand wide in an all-encompassing gesture. "This place is where it's at. Hip, funky, and brimming with life. If you took a walk up the street and actually looked into the buildings rather than dreaming about tearing them down, you'd see a hundred places like this. Jazz bars, tapas bars, Latin American clubs, comedy clubs, and restaurants from all around the world. It's a metropolis of incredible contrasts and I love it."

"You really think I'm some sort of ruthless cretin, don't you?"

He spoke softly and she had to lean forward to hear him over the din of chattering patrons and Spanish guitar music.

Thankfully, the waitress arrived at that moment and deposited two, enormous steaming mugs in front of them, giving her time to phrase her answer carefully. She wanted to be honest, but something about his watchful, brooding expression told her now wasn't the time to be too brutal.

THE CHARMER

"Look, I have this habit of being blunt. You know, honesty is the best policy and all that. Guess I just realised exactly how different we are."

Ariel picked up her latte and took a huge sip, scalding or not. There was honesty and there was *honesty* and from what she'd just said, he might assume she was interested in him. If she burned her tongue on the hot coffee, it mightn't be a bad thing. She might actually shut up for two seconds.

"You got that right," he said, a speculative gleam in his eyes.

Great. The guy wasn't stupid and he'd picked up on her interest just as she'd suspected.

"One more session should see us done," she said, gratefully hiding behind her latte mug.

"Make that two sessions."

"Pardon?"

"One for you, one for me. My business proposal, remember? That one tiny detail you seem to have forgotten?"

"Oh, *that*. You're right, minor details." She smiled, showing she intended no malice. "Maybe I'll be too exhausted after finishing the portrait to hear what you've got to say."

"And maybe I'll spread nasty rumours about the artist getting up close and personal with her model."

"You wouldn't dare."

"Try me."

By his challenging grin, she knew he was kidding, but somehow, she didn't want to test him. Besides, the thought of what he'd suggested sounded way too good to a woman who hadn't got up close and personal with any guy in a long time.

"Do you always get the final word?"

She could've backed down, but where was the fun in that? If there was one thing guaranteed to get her fired up it was a challenge, particularly from a guy who probably always got what he wanted.

Rather than answering her mild dig, he changed the subject altogether.

"You mentioned earlier that all you need to finish is some facial details?"

"Uh-huh."

"Do we have to do that in the studio?"

He reached for his coffee and drained the mug in one go, when what she really wanted to see was his entire face and read where a strange question like that was leading.

"The studio is where I do my portrait work."

Though that wasn't entirely true. She'd often taken a sketch pad down to the St. Kilda foreshore or Albert Park Lake, capturing whatever scene took her fancy, whether it be a person, animal, or landscape. New surroundings inspired her and she loved it.

But the thought of sketching Cooper outside of her studio seemed way too personal.

Like this.

One on one time in a cosy café, sitting across from his sexy smiles and piercing blue eyes, definitely entered the realm of too personal and made her forget one very important point.

This guy was the enemy.

No matter how charming, how glib, how sexy, he was here for one reason and one reason only; to tear her world apart. And she'd be a darn sight smarter to concentrate on that salient fact rather than the intense colour of his eyes.

"Too bad. The weather forecast for the weekend is perfect and I thought it would be good to try a change of scenery. Don't know about you but I need to shake off my moon tan and catch some sun."

He held his chin and turned his face from side to side, a cocky grin on his face. "It would be an excellent opportunity for you to study my exceptional profile in some real light. You know, to put the finishing touches on the masterpiece and all."

She shouldn't encourage him, she really shouldn't. But who could resist a man with a smart mouth like that?

"Where did you have in mind?"

Cooper winked and tapped the side of his nose in true conspirator fashion. "Why don't you leave that up to me? Who knows, this boring hick might surprise you yet. I'll pick you up on Sunday around ten."

With that he stood, took a final glance around the café, sent her a sexy smile and headed out the door, leaving her wondering if she'd taken leave of her senses.

Painting Cooper was one thing. Spending Sunday morning with the cocky, infuriating guy, another.

Think of the finished portrait...think of the money...

Instead, all she could think about was how denim did incredible things to his butt and how stupid she was for noticing. Worse, how in just over a week, she liked this guy more than she'd liked any guy before.

Not good.

And she had a feeling that by spending her precious Sunday morning with him, things were about to get a whole lot worse.

Chapter Fifteen

"Aren't you just full of original ideas this morning?"

Ariel's facetiousness made Cooper chuckle as he held open the door to *Hide*, the funkiest café he could find in Brunswick Street. "Hey, you were the one who said I needed to check out what this precinct has to offer, so here we are."

"Wise guy," she said, her smile warming him better than the sun's rays had for the last hour while he sat on Brighton Beach, more relaxed than he'd been in a long while, as she'd studied his face, her fingers flying over her sketchpad to capture his likeness.

He'd loved the ocean once, had made a weekly trek to some of Victoria's best surf beaches all within a few hours drive from the CBD. However, since starting work at *Vance Corp* he'd been too busy proving himself, putting in the hard yards, to chill out. He wanted to be the best and it came at a price: limited downtime and alienating the one guy who should've been cheering him on rather than hating him for it.

THE CHARMER

"We don't have to do the brunch thing if you don't want to," Ariel said, a tiny frown puckering her forehead as she searched his face for reassurance. "I've got what I needed to finish the portrait so you're obligation-free now."

"Let's eat."

It wasn't her fault his mood had soured courtesy of thoughts of his father's hang ups. Besides, he wanted to make sure this final session ended on a happy note considering the next time they met he'd be pitching his plans for the gallery.

"As long as it's not my head you're biting off," she said, her knowing glance implying she hadn't bought his abrupt brush-off for a second.

"I promise to be nice."

He led the way to the closest table, which happened to be purple and kidney-shaped, boasting lemon vinyl chairs and a cartoon-like backdrop. Like everything else in this street, the *Hide* café was bright, out there, and eclectic.

Ariel fit right in with her denim shorts, indigo silk camisole, and rope espadrilles, whereas he stuck out like a beacon in his conservative navy cargo pants and white T-shirt. Then again, he'd never fit in around here. Orange leather chaps weren't his thing.

"See anything you fancy?"

To his amazement, Ariel blushed and toyed with a long, blonde curl that persistently bounced in the vicinity of her right ear.

"I'll have the mushroom omelette."

"And let me guess. A skinny decaf soy turmeric latte chaser?"

She tilted her nose in the air and sent him an imperious look. "You don't know me at all. I'll have a wheatgrass, orange, and ginger juice please."

The thought of all those ingredients blended together made him want to forego the big fry-up he'd been about to order. "Anyone ever tell you you're a health freak?"

Rather than bristling as he expected, she leaned back against the vinyl booth and chuckled. "I'd rather be a health freak than any other kind of freak."

"You are one interesting woman, Ariel Wallace," he said, locking eyes with her over his menu, wondering if she noticed the growing attraction sizzling between them or it had just been too damn long since he'd dated.

He'd been so busy lately trying to escape his obligations at *Vance Corp* that he'd neglected his social life. Once this deal went through, he'd make sure he remedied that. Though somehow, he had a feeling he'd need quite a few dates with women the antithesis of Ariel to make him forget her.

"Oh yeah, that's me, and I know exactly what you find so interesting about me."

She quirked an eyebrow, full of sass and challenge, and he wondered if he was slipping? Surely his interest in her beauty, her feisty nature, her sharp wit, and her stunning body wasn't that transparent?

He settled for a safe, "What's that?" rather than make a complete fool of himself.

More than he had already, that is.

She snapped her fingers. "You find me interesting because of my gallery. We both know there's no other reason why a guy like you is hanging around a girl like me."

She spoke calmly, without rancour, as if stating an obvious fact. The intriguing part was even though he agreed with her, it rankled.

"You're really into the whole stereotyping thing, aren't you?"

She shrugged. "I'm being honest. No use pretending when we're both grown ups and we know what this is about."

Her hand waved between them, a smooth, flowing, graceful movement demonstrating her artistic side. He loved watching her hands, so full of life and energy and creativity.

"You and I have a business arrangement, Cooper. You've fulfilled your part of the bargain and I'll follow through with mine. So let's just call it what it is and you can save the sweet talk. I'm going to stick to my end of the bargain whether you find me *interesting* or not."

"You don't get compliments very often, do you?"

Which he found incredibly hard to believe considering she was a knockout.

Her green eyes narrowed, as if trying to ascertain if he was serious or toying with her. "Dressed like this and with hair like this?" She plucked at her trendy top and loose curls hanging half way down her back in a frizzy curtain. "What do you think?"

In response, he leaned forward and captured one of those lively, bouncy curls between his thumb and forefinger, rubbing the silky softness. "I think you underestimate yourself. I also think you're beautiful."

For one long, loaded moment she stared at him, her eyes glowing with gratitude and something more, something akin to desire, as a smug, secretive smile curved her lips.

He tugged gently on her curl, leaning forward, knowing what he wanted to do was crazy but unable to stop the gravitational pull towards her.

He wanted to drag her across the table, wrap his arms around her, and kiss her senseless. To taste her rosy lips, to silence her sassy mouth for two seconds and see if his spiralling desire was a figment of his imagination or not.

He didn't think about business or what kissing her could do to his chances for a fair hearing.

He didn't think about tomorrow.

Instead, caught up in the moment, he leaned forward until their faces almost touched. His heart pounded with expectation as Ariel placed her hand square in the middle of his chest and shoved hard, just like she'd pushed him out the door when she first learned his true identity.

"Smooching up to me isn't going to win you any extra points. I said I'll hear you out and I will."

Ariel acted cool but her fiddling hands told him otherwise as they moved from pushing back her hair to adjusting her top to rearranging the cutlery.

Trying to get his ragged breathing under control, he schooled his face into a polite mask, thankful that one of them had kept their cool and furious it hadn't been him.

He needed to wrap this up and fast.

He had no room in his life for emotions.

Because the more time he spent in Ariel's intoxicating company, the more he foundered, and worse, found himself re-evaluating his vows to not get close to anyone.

He had to focus on business.

It was the only way.

"I don't need to score extra points. My proposal will speak for itself." He folded his arms and avoided looking at her mouth, the sexy mouth he'd almost kissed a second ago.

"We'll see, Mr. Big Shot. We'll see."

With an enigmatic smile, she called the waitress over to order, leaving him mulling the wisdom of consorting with the enemy.

Even an enemy as delightful as Ariel.

Chapter Sixteen

Ariel's heart sank as she caught sight of Sofia peering through the gallery's front windows. If the verbose woman caught sight of her with Cooper, goodness knows what might pop out of her gargantuan mouth.

"Who's that?" Cooper said, his long strides making her wish she'd worn flat shoes rather than wedge-heeled espadrilles today. She felt like a toddler running on triple speed to keep up with a giant.

"Sofia Montessori. She's the one who commissioned the portrait."

"I thought she looked familiar. I've seen her at several events."

She should've known a big shot like Cooper would move in similar moneyed circles to Sofia.

Ariel slowed her pace as they neared the front of the gallery, not wanting to get caught up in any name-dropping game that might take place. She hated that sort of thing, which is why she hid in her studio and produced art for people like Sofia and Cooper rather than attend their fancy parties and exhibitions.

She'd been to the occasional party in her early days and hated every minute of it: the yawning cultural and social gap between her and other people, the patronising, condescending attitudes when they discovered she was the artist.

"Hurry. She looks ready to break your door down," Cooper said, shooting her a quizzical look.

"Thanks for walking me back to the gallery but I'm fine, I'll take it from here," she blurted, eager to get rid of him, knowing that any second Sofia would turn her beady gaze their way and have them half way up the aisle before she could say, 'in your dreams.'

"Don't you want me to meet your friend?" A deep frown slashed his brow. "Are you that ashamed to be seen with me?"

If Cooper's warm, friendly persona had scared her, the icy contempt she now heard in his voice terrified her more.

"It's not that. I just want to finish the portrait ASAP and if Sofia lays eyes on you, believe me, she won't leave in a hurry."

He must've been satisfied with her answer because the cold gleam in his eyes softened. "I won't stay. Besides, I've handled worse than Sofia in the business arena and come out unscathed. Trust me."

Shaking her head, she fell into step beside him again. The guy was seriously delusional if he thought she'd trust him with anything. He was here to tear her world apart and all the sexy smiles, gooey eyes, and almost-kisses wouldn't change that.

When they reached the gallery, Ariel took a deep breath and blew it out, hoping to get the introductions out of the way pronto so the woman could be on her way without interrogating her about Cooper.

"Sofia, what are you doing here?" Ariel injected warmth into her voice, knowing she would've been glad to see the lovely woman if Cooper's large, looming presence wasn't at her side.

Sofia stopped peering through the gallery windows and turned. Ariel knew the exact moment she spotted them, because the woman's eyes bulged when they focussed on Cooper.

"*Ciao, bella.*" Sofia kissed both her cheeks before studying Cooper with blatant curiosity, hunger in her gaze. "And who is your friend? He looks awfully familiar."

"Sofia, this is Cooper Vance. Cooper, my friend Sofia Montessori."

"A pleasure, Ms. Montessori." Cooper captured Sofia's hand and bowed over it in an antiquated gesture from years gone by. What a charmer.

He must've known exactly how a woman like Sofia would react, because the older woman preened, simpered, and practically fell in a swooning heap at his feet.

"Ditto, Mr. Vance," Sofia murmured, blushing like a teenager. "Have we met before? I'm positive I've seen you somewhere."

Ariel rolled her eyes, resisting the urge to stick two fingers down her throat and make gagging noises.

"Your reputation in Melbourne society precedes you. Perhaps we've seen each other in passing at a function?"

Sofia's eyes narrowed, her gaze speculative. "No, I don't think so. It's somewhere more recent..."

Ariel wished these two would leave so she could get on with the business of finishing the portrait, obtaining the money, and securing the gallery for another month or so.

But she had to be polite to Sofia, because until she had the commission for the painting in the gallery's bank account, she couldn't afford to offend her.

"Would you like a cup of coffee, Sofia? Cooper was just leaving and I have lots of work to do so we can chat while I paint."

Ariel didn't want Sofia connecting Cooper to the portrait right now. If that happened...

"That's it!" Sofia snapped her fingers and beamed. "You're the model in my portrait." Sofia's hungry gaze travelled the length of Cooper's body while Ariel's heart sank.

Great, just freaking great.

"*Bello*," Sofia murmured, obviously liking what she saw.

Not that Ariel could blame her. Sofia was a red-blooded woman and if she'd admired Ariel's sketches of the man, they were nothing on the real, live model in the flesh. So to speak.

Cooper's brash, unaffected smile made Ariel want to throttle him for being so blasé about the whole situation. "Yes, I'm sitting for Ariel. She's a very talented artist. I think you'll be very pleased with the final result."

"And a nice boy, too," Sofia said, sending Ariel a pointed look as if to say, 'are you crazy to let this guy get away? Why aren't you married by now and expecting his bambino?'

"Speaking of which, I better finish the portrait if you want it by Tuesday—"

"You must come too, Mr. Vance." Sofia's loud voice drowned out a passing tram as she waved her hands in excitement. "Ariel is coming to the little soiree I'm having for my sister's birthday where the portrait will be unveiled and it is only natural that you should attend also."

"No," Ariel blurted before she could stop herself, blushing furiously when two sets of eyes turned on her,

Sofia's knowing brown eyes and Cooper's dazzling blue. "I mean, I'm sure Cooper has better things to do with his time. Besides, he'd probably be mortified if people recognise him as the model. He's a businessman and it wouldn't look good."

Ariel babbled, giving Cooper the evil eye, silently praying he'd back her up on this. She didn't want him anywhere near that party. They'd spent enough time socialising, what with coffee on Friday night and brunch today. The longer she spent with him, the more befuddled she became, and she needed her wits about her to fob him off after listening to his stupid proposal.

Liking someone and enjoying their company wasn't conducive to kicking their butt out the door, and that's exactly what she'd have to do after hearing his pitch.

So no more socialising.

Starting now.

"What do you think, Mr. Vance?" Sofia frowned at Ariel before flashing a charming smile at Cooper.

"I think it's a great idea." Cooper's challenging stare made Ariel's right foot twitch to kick his sexy butt. "Thanks for the invitation."

"*Bene.* That's settled. Now, why don't we go in and I can give you the details?"

Ignoring Sofia's triumphant grin and Cooper's smug smile, Ariel sighed in resignation and unlocked the front door.

Two against one wasn't fair.

But then, since when had anything in her life been fair?

Chapter Seventeen

"I should never have agreed to this," Ariel muttered at her reflection, wishing she could wield a mascara wand with the same expertise as a paint brush.

She'd never gone in for makeup. She much preferred painting canvases than painting her face. Then again, tonight called for a confidence mask, and if the barest foundation, sheer blue eye-shadow, a quick lashing of mascara, and pale pink lip gloss would help quell the butterflies dancing a tango in her belly, she'd use it.

Seeing Cooper at Sofia's charity event was one thing but agreeing to accompany him? Madness.

Right on cue, a knock at the front door had her casting one last regretful glance at her reflection in the mirror before she picked up her embroidered silver evening purse and flicked off the lights.

Though how hard could tonight be? She'd wait around for the portrait unveiling, make polite small talk with a bunch of rich phoneys, then bolt back here in a taxi, leaving Cooper with his cronies.

Easy.

However, the moment she opened the door and saw Cooper wearing a designer tux and a sexy smile, she knew nothing about this evening would be easy. The way her pulse accelerated and her heart flip-flopped, nothing could be further from the truth.

"You look beautiful."

His soft, almost reverent voice strummed her skin like a gentle caress and she shivered with delight that she could evoke a reaction like that from a guy like him as he stepped into the doorway, blocking out the sounds of busy Brunswick Street, and took hold of her hand.

"It's vintage," she said, a totally inane remark as she stood frozen, her hand captured in his, enjoying the physical contact way too much.

"It suits you."

The admiration in his appreciative gaze made her hold onto his hand too long and she sighed in relief when he released it. Short-lived, because once his hand was free, he skimmed his palm over the sheer chiffon of her dress cascading in handkerchief layers from her waist to the floor.

"You look like a beautiful waterfall. Fresh, vibrant, invigorating."

"And you need to move into the twenty-first century," she said, disarmed by his charm. "With lines like that, I'm not surprised you spend all your time with your head buried behind a computer."

She didn't mean to sound so cutting but she didn't handle compliments well. Especially compliments from a guy standing way too close and smelling like a dream.

To her surprise, he chuckled rather than rebuke her. "You're not going to spoil tonight with that smart mouth of yours. Insult me all you like but I'm not biting."

More's the pity.

He smirked as if reading her mind and she propelled him out the door, anything to put some much needed distance between them. Even seated in his car would be better than having him invade her personal space. Not that she minded exactly, but if they didn't get a move on, she'd be tempted to rush back into the gallery, slip into shorts and a poncho, and have a TV dinner while watching her favourite DIY house renovation show.

Boring but safe. The complete antithesis of allowing Cooper to drape her hand in the crook of his elbow and lead her to his low-slung sports car parked around the corner.

Exciting and dangerous. Yeah, that was Cooper through and through and for a girl who liked being dull and safe she was enticed at the prospect of living a little for once.

"Flash car," she said, sliding into the plush, leather interior as he held the passenger door open for her.

"It was a gift."

She looked at him in surprise, his abrupt tone implying he didn't like it. Or maybe didn't like the person who had given it to him?

As he slid behind the wheel, started the engine, and pulled away from the curb, she couldn't resist probing further. "Let me guess. Daddy bought it for you as a bonus last year?"

"Close," he said, his voice tight, his hands clenched on the steering wheel.

She could've left it there but she didn't. After being ignored for the first eight years of her life as she flitted from orphanage to foster home and back again, living with Barb had opened a whole new world to her. Barb had encouraged her natural curiosity, had answered her endless questions with the patience of a saint.

Ariel loved mystery novels for that very reason, always

wanting questions answered, the unsolvable unravelled, and right now, she had a doozy of a puzzle laid out before her and there was no way she could back down.

"Pretty generous gift. You two must be close to whoever gave it to you."

"We were."

Cooper's use of past tense could only mean two things; they'd fallen out or worse, the other person was dead. Maybe she should quell her curiosity and keep her mouth shut.

"My father gave me the car. We don't get along these days," Cooper said, his icy tone sending chills down her spine.

"I'm sorry."

Her apology extended beyond her probing. How could she contemplate for one second that she could make tonight work? Even when she was trying to fit in, she made a mess of things. Rather than keeping the conversation light, she'd pushed for answers, nosing around where she didn't belong.

"So am I." Cooper didn't say anymore and this time, she didn't push, clamping her glossed lips tightly shut and staring out the window at the glittering lights of Melbourne as they wound their way to Toorak, one of the city's richest suburbs.

However, after five minutes passed and the uncomfortable silence yawned between them, she said, "Do you have any music?"

"Sure." He touched a fancy keypad that looked like it could launch the space shuttle until muted jazz filled the car. "How's that?"

"Not bad," she said, hoping for something more upbeat. Anything to lighten the mood.

"What sort of music do you like?"

"Latin American. Flamenco. Anything with a bit of oomph."

The exact opposite of his boring choice, but she wisely kept that to herself.

However, he zoned in on her thoughts with unerring accuracy once again. "You think I'm some kind of business-oriented bore, don't you?"

Got it in one, Coop.

However, in the interests of making the rest of the drive and the hour or so of torture she had ahead of her at the party bearable, she chose her words carefully. "We're different, that's all."

"Like opposites attracting?"

"Who said anything about attraction?"

She kept her tone deliberately light, knowing she'd successfully stepped through one verbal minefield only to plough straight into another. A more dangerous minefield this time, one with the potential to detonate and leave her heart in tiny, shattered fragments if she acknowledged her growing attraction for this guy.

"Come on, tell me the truth. I've seen how you look at me when you're painting."

"What a load of—"

His laughter drowned out the rest of her response and she reluctantly joined in, recognising she'd been duped and how he'd effectively lightened the mood.

"Okay, now that I can add enormous ego to the list of your faults, you better quit while you're behind."

He chuckled. "So you're fixated on my behind too, huh?"

Shooting him a glare that could melt wax, the scorching glance he fired right back surprised her. Thankfully, they were stopped at traffic lights, otherwise the heat they created with that one locked stare could've made him ram a light pole.

With a superior smile, she said, "The way I observed your body was purely professional. Anything else you imagine you saw is pure speculation on your part. Incorrect speculation I might add."

He laughed and refocussed on the road as the lights changed to green, his deep, rich laughter rolling over her like low-lying clouds on a sultry summer's day. "Come on, Ariel, admit it. You want my body."

"I want your head on a platter, preferably with an apple stuffed in that big mouth of yours."

To her annoyance, heat crawled under her skin, setting her nerve endings alight with longing.

He was right, damn him.

She did want his body.

Looking-but-not-touching had driven her slowly but surely mad over the last two weeks. The more time they spent together, the more quips they traded, the more they laughed, she knew it wasn't just his magnificent body she wanted.

His mind attracted her too.

The same mind that is busily hatching plots to snatch the gallery and your life away from you.

How gullible could she be?

"On that note, we're here," he said, pulling into a long, tree-lined driveway boasting enough expensive vehicles to keep car thieves rolling in wealth until the next century.

Men in prim, black uniforms rushed about like hyperactive penguins, opening car doors, taking keys, and keeping the long line of vehicles moving at a steady pace past the imposing double doors at the front of the house, thrown open to let light from a crystal chandelier spill onto the marble tiled entry porch.

Ariel unconsciously reached for a curl to twist around her finger, forgetting she'd piled most of them on top of her head in a poor imitation of a posh up-do.

This place made her feel gauche.

From the ostentatious cream-rendered, double storey house that sprawled across the large block, the flood-lit tennis court she glimpsed behind the house to the right, and the hand-trimmed topiary trees that looked like a real, live zoo leading up to the entrance, every self-preserving instinct told Ariel to make a run for it.

People who lived in places like this, who drove cars like the ones lining the drive, who attended parties like this, meant one thing to her.

Trouble.

She'd battled the prejudices of rich people her entire life and despite how far she'd come, she hated the feelings evoked as they looked down their aristocratic noses at the scruffy, weird artist like she hadn't risen out of the gutter far enough.

She didn't think she had a hang-up about her past but whenever she got within two feet of a patronising snob, all her old insecurities rushed back and left her feeling inadequate.

"What's wrong?" Cooper had put the car into Park mode and turned to face her, a frown lining his forehead.

"This isn't my scene."

Her hand fluttered to her face, searching for that elusive curl to twirl in comfort and coming up empty again.

Great, the one time that lousy curl behaved itself and actually stayed tucked up and off her face she had the urge to rip it down and twist it around and around her finger.

"Consider it part of your job," he said, his voice soft and soothing. "This is networking at its best, where you get to scope out potential customers, feed them what they want to hear, and promote your business. And if all else fails, fall back on the old standard."

"What's that?"

"Picture the lot of them naked."

She managed a tight smile, grateful for his presence and the support he offered. It would've been much harder to attend this soiree alone, yet with Cooper, one of their own, she could blend into the background without too much difficulty.

"Anyone ever tell you you've got a fixation for the naked human form?"

"That's you, sweetheart, not me." He reached out and squeezed her hand, a brief, impersonal touch but supportive nonetheless, and she could've kissed him for it.

Though she wouldn't go there...not if she knew what was good for her.

"Ready to go in?"

"Ready as I'll ever be," she muttered, tugging on her tight bodice and patting the top of her head tentatively to see if her thick, unmanageable mop was still in place.

"Remember, think naked," he said, giving her a heart-stopping grin before releasing her hand and stepping out of the car.

"It's show-time," she murmured, feeling more like a supporting actress than the star attraction and hoping she wouldn't fluff her lines.

Ironically, the hoity-toity crowd wasn't the only thing that had her stomach roiling with nerves. The thought she might make a fool of herself with Cooper, whose opinion she'd come to care way too much about, made her feel sick.

Absurd, to care so much about his opinion of her, and the sooner tonight was over, he delivered his pitch, and he exited her life, the better off she'd be.

Then why the scary, empty feeling at the thought?

Chapter Eighteen

Cooper schmoozed for business all the time and had faking it in social settings down to an art, so attending this soiree should've been easy.

Instead, he'd been on guard ever since he got out of the car and had stayed close to Ariel as they walked the path towards the imposing double doors of the mansion. She'd been oddly vulnerable in the car, at complete odds with her usual feistiness, and he wanted to put her at ease. He also wanted her next to him for a purely selfish reason; he liked having her there.

The quirky, sassy woman had him laughing more than he had in ages and he enjoyed firing right back at her. Not to mention the way her unique green eyes sparkled with cheeky glee when she scored a direct hit with her teasing barbs.

However, spending time with Ariel had one major drawback; he had to keep reminding himself of the real reason, the only reason, he was with her.

Business.

He'd never lost sight of the ultimate goal in any deal and

he wouldn't start now. Not when leaving *Vance Corporation* was all important.

He'd had enough of his dad and his tyrannical style of running a company. Time to get away, start up some healthy competition, and see if that made the old man sit up and take notice.

"Uh-oh, look at all these people." Ariel gripped his arm tighter and all but yanked him behind a marble pillar as they stepped into an elaborate foyer.

"Hey, didn't my pep talk in the car resonate?"

He refrained from patting her hand, knowing she'd probably slug him on the nose for being patronising.

She shook her head and the pile of curls piled on the top wobbled, enveloping him in a bizarre fruity-floral scent he'd yet to identify and was too embarrassed to ask her about. The same scent that haunted him, enticed him, and beckoned him to get closer to her.

"Sorry, the naked visualisation thing doesn't do it for me."

"Even after seeing me with my clothes off?"

She rolled her eyes but at least he saw a glimmer of a smile. "Especially after that."

"Ouch, you sure know how to wound a guy's ego." He clutched his heart in mock pain, eliciting more of a smile from her enticing mouth coated in a shiny gloss.

He'd never seen her wear makeup, and her subtle use of cosmetics tonight highlighted her exquisite features to perfection.

"With the size of ego a big shot like you has, I seriously doubt that."

Shaking his head and exceedingly pleased his distraction technique had worked, he said, "I take it the big shot label isn't a term of endearment?"

THE CHARMER

Her smile faded. "It's a fact. You're a businessman, I'm an artist. You want something I have, which is the only reason you're here tonight and being so darn nice to me. So let's go in, do the obligatory social niceties, and get out of here before this princess turns into a pumpkin."

"Fine," he said, not sure what annoyed him more: how little she thought of him or the element of truth behind her brutal honesty.

"Fine," she echoed, tilting her head up like a queen and marching away, leaving him with a tantalising view of a straight, bare back courtesy of her daring dress, while the rest of it cascaded from her waist to the floor in shimmery shades of aquamarine, turquoise, and emerald, the exact colour of the Great Barrier Reef on a clear day.

So much for a connection. He tried to be nice and what did he get for his trouble? An earful. He tried to be rational about this business deal between them and what did he get? Angst.

And she hadn't even heard his pitch yet.

He'd never pretended he was anything but the heartless tycoon she thought he was. Business meant everything to him. It was all he knew.

He'd blitzed his uni degrees, waltzed into a cushy job, and proceeded to set the business world alight. He deserved to be confident. Failure wasn't in his vocabulary. Never had been, never would be.

And no matter how stubborn the eccentric Miss Wallace wanted to be, he'd make sure he wouldn't fail this time.

He couldn't. There was too much at stake.

Chapter Nineteen

"You are enjoying yourself, *bella*, yes?"

Ariel took a sip of her sparkling mineral water, not wanting to lie to Sofia, yet needing a few seconds to compose an honest but graceful answer.

"Everyone seems to be having a wonderful time," Ariel said, knowing it sounded lame and the astute Sofia would pick up on it in a second.

She did.

"I do not care for everyone else, *bella*. What about you? Are you all right?"

Ariel nodded and forced a smile, hoping it didn't look like a grimace. "I guess I'm just tired after rushing the portrait."

Sofia beamed. "Ah, yes, the portrait. It is magnificent. Maria loves it."

"And seems to be infatuated with the model."

Ariel inclined her head towards Sofia's sister, who for a woman of forty looked fifteen years younger in a siren red poured-on dress, luscious dark hair that hung in perfect waves to her shoulders, and huge, expressive brown eyes firmly fixed on Cooper, along with her talon-like hands gripping his arm as she smiled at him.

"So that's what is troubling you..." Sofia waved her hand towards Maria in an abrupt, dismissive gesture. "Don't be jealous, *bella*, she is no competition to you."

Ariel stiffened, not liking Sofia's implication. She'd have to care to be jealous and she didn't. Caring about Cooper would be akin to skipping into the dentist with a big, goofy grin on her face and clapping her hands with glee: pure and utter madness.

"I'm not interested in Cooper, so you can get that maniacal matchmaking gleam out of your eyes," Ariel said, her stern glare having little effect.

Predictably, Sofia ignored her. "How can you not be interested? The man is handsome, successful, charming, cultured—"

"And out to ruin me."

Ariel glared at Cooper through narrow eyes, wondering why he let himself be pawed. Didn't the guy have any dignity?

Considering how fast he'd whipped off his clothes to insinuate his way into her good graces, probably not.

"Maybe you should listen to him, see what he has to say about the gallery, before jumping to conclusions?"

Sofia's tone had softened and Ariel knew that while she meant well, her friend didn't have a clue.

"That so-called charming man probably wants to kick me out of the gallery, tear it down, and erect some awful monstrosity that won't fit in with Brunswick Street." She shook her head. "I've been fobbing off his kind ever since Aunt Barb died. He's not the first and he won't be the last but one thing I'm sure of, I'm not leaving. I promised Aunt Barb."

Sofia laid a comforting hand on her arm, patting it gently. "Babs would've wanted you to be happy. She was one of my closest friends and I know how much she loved you, how much joy you brought to her life. She would want the same for you."

Sofia paused, as if searching for the right words. "Instead, you're working too hard, battling to keep the gallery open. You won't accept help from anyone and you bristle like some feral cat whenever anyone offers. Perhaps it is time to reconsider?"

"No."

The concern in Sofia's dark eyes hardened Ariel's resolve. She didn't want to reconsider anything. She'd made a promise to Aunt Barb and she'd do her best to keep it. She had no other option.

Her promise was all she'd been able to offer Aunt Barb in return for years of unswerving love and support, and there was no way she would break it, even if it meant taking on ten extra jobs. Or doing ten more life portraits as much as she hated them.

Though if all the models looked like Cooper...

Mentally slapping herself for even going there, she enveloped Sofia in a hug. "I'm sorry for snapping at you. I know you mean well but I have to do this my way."

Sofia pulled back and patted her cheek. "In that case, why don't you go and mingle? Several people have expressed interest in getting portraits done by the fabulous artist who painted Maria's birthday present. And of course, the men are all dying to meet the gorgeous creature in the stunning green dress."

Ariel glanced down at the fitted bodice, spaghetti straps,

and pointy panelled, flowing chiffon of her vintage dress. With all the couture in this room, they thought this dress is stunning? It proved her point about what a bunch of phoneys this rich crowd was.

However, obtaining a few more commissions could mean the difference between keeping the gallery open for another year or not, and though she hated the patronising, condescending atmosphere in the room, she'd swallow her pride and think of *Colour by Dreams*.

"You're not pushing them in my direction I hope?"

Sofia threw her hands up in theatrical despair. "How could you think such a thing?" She winked and gave Ariel a none-too-gentle shove towards the main throng gathered at the floor-to-ceiling French doors opening out onto a sandstone paved patio. "Now go."

"I'm going, I'm going," Ariel muttered, downing the rest of her sparkling water and wishing she liked the taste of champagne. A little false courage wouldn't go astray. She hated marketing, particularly self promotion.

Not surprising, considering she'd spent the first eight years of her life trying to fade into the background at the various orphanages, foster homes, and during that interminable week-long stint on the streets.

Falling asleep in an old canvas in Barb's backyard had been the luckiest break of her life. Now, if only her luck could hold...for the next twenty years or so.

"Going somewhere?"

A hand clamped on her arm out of nowhere and she stopped, shrugging off Cooper's grip before speaking.

"I'm off to do some networking, like some business guru advised me on the way over here."

Cooper grinned and she wished her heart wouldn't do that weird little tango whenever he did. "You mean you're actually listening to me? And better yet, taking my advice?"

"Yeah, go figure? I must be drunk."

"On that clear sparkling stuff you've been drinking for the last hour? I doubt it."

A small part of Ariel was flattered he'd managed to tear his gaze away from fawning Maria for more than a second to notice what she'd been drinking, while a larger part—the logical part—told her she was crazy for caring.

"Look, why don't you head back to your friends and let me continue doing what I have to do?" *And the only reason why I came here in the first place.* "In fact, once I finish chatting to a few people I'll never see again if I'm lucky, I'm heading home, so thanks for the ride."

His smile vanished and his eyes darkened to a stormy midnight. "Firstly, these people aren't my friends. They're acquaintances, and the main reason I'm here is to support you, not party with people I barely know. Secondly, I'm not some immature young man you can give the brush off to when it suits you. I brought you, I'll take you home." He glowered. "And lastly, in case you didn't know, this whole 'woe-is-me' act of yours is wearing a little thin. You're out of your depth here? Well, listen up, sweetheart. Everyone gets that feeling, from the Prime Minister to garbage collectors. You're a big girl, deal with it. Now off you go, show these people half the spunk you show me and when you're ready, I'll meet you outside."

Ariel stared at Cooper in stunned disbelief as he strode through the open French doors without looking back, torn between wanting to run after him and give him a clip around the ears for speaking to her like that and doing exactly as he said; make this crowd notice her, make some contacts, promote her business, no matter how much she hated it and how far out of her depth she felt.

Woe-is-me act?

"I'll show him," she muttered, glaring daggers in Cooper's direction and squaring her shoulders to shake up this crowd.

Chapter Twenty

Ariel flounced ahead of Cooper into the studio, not bothering to turn on lights, other than the two elephant lamps she'd picked up for a bargain at a local vintage sale. "You do know the only reason I let you drive me home was because I couldn't get a taxi or Uber for half an hour?"

"I didn't think it was for my scintillating company, considering you didn't speak and pouted the whole way."

"I didn't pout."

"No? Then what's that pursing thing you're doing with your lips right now?"

Before she could blink, Cooper leaned forward, his thumb gently brushing her lips, eliciting a tingle spread that throughout her body, lingering in places that hadn't tingled in a long while.

"Nothing to say?" He smirked. "That's a first."

Ariel couldn't speak if she wanted to. Her tongue was glued to the roof of her mouth at the sheer shock of being touched by Cooper as if he desired her, as if she was more than the enemy to him.

THE CHARMER

Besides, she was too scared to speak. If she opened her mouth, there was no telling what she might do with his thumb in the vicinity of her mouth, her main impulse being to nibble it.

His thumb skidded across her bottom lip and drifted lower, tracing a slow, leisurely path along her jaw and back, making her knees wobble and her body sway towards him.

"Guess I better go before you ply me with any of your herbal concoctions, huh?" He cupped her cheek, his hypnotic stare mesmerising, as if the last thing he wanted to do was leave.

Or was that her misguided interpretation? Was she wishing for something that wasn't there, considering he made her feel like a desirable woman, an equal, someone he admired?

When he touched her like this, looked at her like this, she could almost forget the huge, yawning gap between them, a gap that attending the party tonight only reinforced.

Cooper belonged in the rich, uppity crowd she would've shunned given half a chance, and she didn't. She never would, and that was fine by her. He knew it, she knew it, so what was this tender act about?

In that moment, it hit her.

The proposal.

Cooper, a ruthless businessman, would probably do anything to get what he wanted.

She'd had a plan for when he dropped her home. Give him a chance to deliver his almighty proposal, refuse, send him away, and concentrate on sorting through the business cards that had been discreetly palmed her way this evening. Sofia had been right. People were interested in her painting, though realistically, even if she worked night and day for the next few months, the commissions wouldn't stave off the inevitable.

She needed money, a lot of it, to keep the gallery running, and right now, with Cooper staring at her with a speculative gleam in his too-blue eyes, reminding her exactly why he was here, she knew she was fast running out of options.

Discombobulated by his touch, she was about to shove him away when he lowered his hand, regret etched across his striking face.

"Mind telling me what that was all about?"

"I think you know," he said, his gaze travelling over her from head to foot, slowly, lingering, making her shiver with need as if his hands had skimmed a similar trail. "But until you're willing to admit this attraction between us exists, I'm not going to do anything about it."

He held up his hand before she could protest. "And no, before you belittle it, pretend it doesn't exist, or imply I'm schmoozing you to get close to you to undermine you, this buzz between us has nothing to do with business and everything to do with the way you drive me crazy."

For the second time this evening, Cooper left her gobsmacked as he walked away.

Chapter Twenty-One

Cooper finished reading the last page of the proposal, returned it to the stack of papers in front of him, and slipped a copy into a presentation folder.

This was it.

D-day. Developer day, when he convinced Ariel to sign over the gallery, guaranteeing him a new start away from his cantankerous father.

The documentation was flawless and he'd planned for every contingency.

Apart from the one where she said no to his immaculately laid out plans.

Though that wouldn't happen if Ariel knew what was good for her, and after spending time with the bohemian beauty, he knew for a fact that Ariel's brain was as impressive as the rest of her. Something his father would've recognised if he hadn't barged into this deal with all the finesse of a wounded rhino.

Then again, Eric hadn't even rated Ariel, preferring to deal through the council that held her lease.

A small part of Cooper wished his father had sealed this deal because that would've given him free reign to pursue Ariel, to explore the sizzling attraction between them, to kiss her...

He'd been tempted last night, so close to throwing his ideals to the wind, hauling her into his arms, and making every fantasy he'd ever had about her come true. Thankfully, his befuddled brain had kicked into gear at the last minute and he'd averted a mini disaster.

As much as he wanted Ariel, he wanted to get out of *Vance Corporation* more and make his stubborn old coot of a dad wake up.

"Got a minute?"

Speak of the devil...

Eric strode into the office without waiting for an invite and stood over Cooper's desk.

"Sure, what's up?"

It irked Cooper that he couldn't call Eric 'dad' in the office. They'd dropped the 'dad' and 'son' act as soon as he joined the company. Sad but true.

Cooper had worked hard, putting in long hours, nailing the big deals, doing more for *Vance Corporation* than any other employee in the company's history, all in the vain hope that his father would treat him like a valued asset, or better, the son he'd once loved.

No more. He was done wishing for something that would never eventuate.

Eric crossed his arms. "What's the deal with the Wallace woman? Have you signed her yet?" He tapped his watch. "We're due to meet with the investors in a few days."

Cooper pointed at the document folder in front of him. "I'm meeting with her in an hour."

THE CHARMER

An ugly sneer creased Eric's face. "That's just dandy, but is she going to sign on the dotted line?"

"I'm confident." Cooper kept his answers short, non-confrontational, just like he'd learned to do because of his dad's short temper.

Eric glanced away, oddly uncomfortable, before eyeballing him. "What will you do then?"

Cooper stared at his dad in confusion. They'd never talked beyond the deal. Cooper knew the day he delivered the signed documentation was the day he walked out of here with his contract in tatters, but his father had never asked about his future plans. Eric was rarely interested in anything but himself.

"Do you really want to know?"

To his surprise, Eric slumped into the chair opposite and lost the surly expression. "Yeah, I do. You've worked here ever since university, I think I'm entitled to know your plans."

"As my ex-employer or as my father?"

Cooper almost spat the words even though he knew now wasn't the time or place to have the in-depth father/son chat he'd craved for the last year. He had more important things to focus on, like convincing a crazy artist to hand over her studio.

"Guess I deserved that."

If Cooper had been surprised by his father's question, Eric's concerned expression floored him. For a moment, it almost appeared like his dad cared.

"Look, Coop, things have been pretty full-on around here for the last year. Maybe I've taken you for granted. You're a good worker. You'll go places." Eric's expression hardened. "Seems a shame to throw it all away on a whim."

A *whim*? His father thought Cooper's dream of starting his own company was nothing more than a whim?

Cooper's tiny flicker of hope extinguished. His dad wasn't interested in re-establishing a father/son bond. He wasn't interested in making up for lost time, for all the months they'd wasted dancing around one another.

Uh-uh, his dad was only concerned about his precious business.

Cooper should've known.

He stood abruptly, shrugged into his suit jacket, and picked up the presentation folder. "Thanks for the vote of confidence, but this isn't a whim. Striking out on my own is something I have to do. You'd understand that if you knew me."

Cooper ignored the hurt in his father's eyes and walked out the door, his attention already focussed on the meeting ahead and its importance for his future.

Chapter Twenty-Two

Ariel flitted around the studio, lighting lime and tangerine candles, plumping the sequinned purple cushions on the ruby sofas, and tidying up the evidence of her nerves.

She'd drunk a dozen cups of chamomile tea since calling Cooper this morning to let him know today was as good a time as any to hear his pitch. But now, as she stacked the cups in the dishwasher and made her umpteenth visit to the toilet, she wondered if she'd done the right thing.

'Keep your friends close and your enemies closer' had been one of Barb's favourite sayings so Ariel had taken the plunge and called him, despite her stomach still churning since their almost-kiss last night.

If she'd had her way, she would've never laid eyes on Cooper again but they'd made a deal; he'd upheld his end of the bargain and now it was her turn.

Glancing around the studio, her heart swelled with pride. Sunlight streamed through the soaring windows, filtering through the colourful gauze swaths of chiffon she'd hung from curtain hooks, casting a warm, rainbow over the room. Combined with the refreshing tang of citrus from the aromatherapy candles, and the bright ruby and amethyst colour combination of the furniture against the polished oak boards, the place looked inviting: warm, welcoming, a haven.

Her haven. It had been from the minute she set foot in this room, a scared and starving eight year old who thought she'd stepped into a fairytale treasure cave. The colours had bewitched her, the cosiness had beckoned, and Barb had set her up with an easel and paints like she belonged here.

Thanks to Aunt Barb, that feeling hadn't waned over the years. If anything, it had intensified, to the point she couldn't see herself living and working anywhere else. *Colour by Dreams* had made all hers come true.

It meant everything to her.

She wanted Cooper to view the studio how she saw it, to feel its ambience, to recognise how much it meant to her.

This wasn't just about her fervent promise to Aunt Barb. This was her home, the only home she'd ever known, and she would fight with everything she had to hold onto it.

The wind chimes over the gallery front door tinkled and Ariel took a deep breath, wondering what made her more nervous: rejecting Cooper's pitch or seeing him so soon after he'd almost made her swoon like the women whose vintage clothes she favoured.

"Ariel?"

"Be right there," she called out, casting one last frantic gaze around the studio and wondering if it was too late to wear her lucky garland.

Though it would clash terribly with her flowing, floral dress cinched at the waist with a crocheted macramé belt, and pink flip-flops. Not that she usually cared, revelling in combining colours, patterns, fabrics, and shoes with creative abandon, but she'd told Cooper about the garland's significance and didn't want him prying further.

Crossing her fingers behind her back that after hearing Cooper's pitch she wouldn't want to tear his eyes out, she pushed through the beaded curtain.

"Right on time." She injected enthusiasm into her voice. "This business meeting must be important to you."

"It is."

Her tone had been light and flippant, his was anything but. Combined with his charcoal designer suit, white shirt, burgundy tie, and an expression that could've frozen ice in Antarctica, he looked ready for business. Serious business.

Ironic, considering she could've sworn he'd had monkey business on his mind when last here.

"Go through to the studio and I'll flip the lunch sign. How long is this going to take?"

"Not long if you're sensible about it."

Ariel's narrow-eyed glare was lost on Cooper as he strode past her and into the studio.

She waited for some recognition of her efforts, some small comment that he appreciated the beauty of the room, but after locking the gallery door, flipping the sign, and heading back into the studio, one look at the grim expression on his handsome face told her she'd prettied up the place for nothing.

He didn't get it.

Not that she should be surprised. Despite the teasing chats, the traded barbs, and the light-hearted banter they'd exchanged, Cooper embodied the cold-hearted businessman she'd labelled him as soon as she'd learned his identity.

He'd dulled her senses with his nice act and foolishly, she'd let him.

"Have a seat," she said, trying to quell the rampaging butterflies in her gut and failing. "Would you like a drink?"

"No thanks."

He barely looked at her, rifling through a huge, scary black folder in his hands before pulling out an equally scary wad of paper.

"If you're planning to bamboozle me with a lot of facts and figures about projections and land values, forget it. Just give me the basics."

She plopped onto one of the sofas, kicked off her flip-flops, and curled her feet under her. Though her insides churned with dread, she needed to present a cool, calm façade, and making herself comfortable was part of that. Maybe she should invite this new, uptight version of Cooper to slip out of his shoes and take a load off too?

She smothered a giggle at the thought.

"I'm glad to see you in such a good mood," he said, shooting her a quizzical look as he perched on the opposite end of the sofa, as far away from her physically as he could get without sliding onto the floor in an undignified heap.

"Let's keep it that way," she said, pasting a confident smile on her face when in reality she desperately needed to make another mad dash to the toilet.

He didn't return her smile. In fact, he didn't do much of anything. His face appeared carved out of granite, his blue eyes cold and flat like Port Phillip Bay on a frigid winter's day.

She'd known he had this side to him. This was probably the real Cooper and the nice side he'd been showing her had been part of his elaborate plan to loosen her up in preparation for this day.

She'd been a fool.

But then again, what had she lost apart from a few

nights' sleep while dreaming the most amazing, erotic dreams of her life over a model with a body to die for and an artist who'd turned to sculpting and had her hands all over him?

"So you want the basics?" He asked, his expression grim.

"Uh-huh."

"Okay." He laid down his hefty sheaf of papers on the coffee table in front of them and turned to face her, those chilly, lifeless eyes scaring her more than the pitch she didn't want to hear.

"This gallery is on land that is leased and that lease is coming up for renewal shortly. Apparently, Barbara Vann, who signed the original lease, signed it for twenty-five years and in doing so, effectively gave you control after she passed away."

He took a quick breath and continued. "You have refused previous offers to vacate the property but it will be in your best interest to consider accepting the offer I've set out in the documentation. Otherwise, once the lease runs out, you may find you have no option but to leave with nothing, as the council can re-lease or sell to anyone they please."

Ariel stared at Cooper in growing horror, hearing every cold, callous word he uttered, wishing she didn't understand. However, she did, all too well.

She'd known about the lease being up for renewal shortly but she'd assumed the council would be happy to renegotiate with her. After all, she was a good tenant. She paid her rent on time—mostly. She didn't cause trouble—apart from that one, tiny fire in the storeroom that technically wasn't her fault.

Besides, the council always supported local ventures,

encouraging the alternative, hip vibe that made Brunswick Street unique. Big Shot Cooper was just trying to scare her into giving him what he wanted and she wouldn't budge.

She would continue to make *Colour by Dreams* one of Melbourne's most prominent galleries—if she scraped up enough money over the next few months to pay her skyrocketing overheads—and face the lease renewal when it came up.

"By that horrified look on your face, I'm guessing you're not too keen on the idea."

Ariel tucked her legs tighter and folded her arms, inadequate defence mechanisms against the onslaught of trouble she faced. "Your powers of deduction are amazing. I'm not surprised you're such a shark."

"Don't." Cooper stood abruptly and strode to a window, his gaze fixed on some faraway spot, though what he found so intriguing about the run-down fence, the back neighbour's rusted chimney flue, or the pile of old easels, she'd never know.

"Don't what? Call it how it is? Throw in a little sarcasm to lighten the mood?" She unfolded her legs in one, smooth movement and stood, joining him at the window to gaze out at the tiny, square patch of backyard, the same patch she'd curled up in eighteen years earlier on that freezing winter's night when she'd been so famished, so light-headed, she hadn't been able to take another step. "Come on, you've had your fun, let me have mine."

"This is a business proposal. It's not personal," he said, not turning to acknowledge her, not moving a muscle.

Not personal? She could happily punch him in the nose for that. Everything about this low deal was personal.

Taking away her home? Personal.

Ruining her dreams? Personal.

THE CHARMER

Making her break a promise to the one woman who had taken a chance on her? Personal.

Destroying her plans to continue Barb's work in fostering local talent and helping street kids like she'd once been? Personal, personal, *personal*.

Whirling to face him, she grabbed hold of his arm, forcing him to look at her. "You don't get it, do you? Look around. Tell me what you see."

She finally got a reaction out of him, a tiny frown indenting his forehead.

"Do it," she said, tugging on his arm when he didn't move. "Go on, describe what you see."

After a long pause, he turned to face the studio and she released his arm, determinedly ignoring the heat scorching her palm.

"I see a large room. Polished floorboards. Two red sofas. Sparkly cushions. Heaps of art stuff. Curtains made of a fancy material."

His flat, deadpan voice suited his flat, deadpan description perfectly and her heart sank further.

She'd known they were worlds apart with little common ground, but she'd hoped he might have developed some aesthetic sense over the last few weeks, some idea of what how she felt about this place.

She'd been wrong.

About everything.

Including her warped feelings that she might actually like this guy, and once she knocked back his stupid business proposal, they might actually have a chance at being more than friends.

Right now, even friends seemed out of the question, and it hurt more than it should.

"What else do you see?" She urged, giving him one last

chance to show her he understood where she was coming from, where she was going.

"Tiny kitchenette, elephant lamps, candles, art magazines." He turned to her, his expectant expression like a pupil expecting praise from a teacher.

Praise? In his case, he'd just scored a big, fat F.

"You would see that," she muttered, turning away from him and crossing the room so he wouldn't see the sudden tears filling her eyes.

She never cried, yet the harder she blinked them away, the more tears swelled in her eyes until they overflowed and ran down her cheeks in pitiful rivulets.

"I'm not sure I understand."

Thankfully, Cooper's voice came from near the windows indicating he hadn't moved.

She didn't want him to see her like this.

She wouldn't give him the satisfaction.

"I didn't think you would," she murmured, holding back the sobs that threatened. "Just go. Leave the proposal. I'll consider it and get back to you."

"But I need an answer—"

"I don't care what you need. Please leave and lock the door behind you."

Her voice quavered and she bit down on her bottom lip, hating him for making her feel this vulnerable, this weak.

"I'll call you," he said, his footsteps echoing on the polished boards as he left the studio, the soft tinkling of the wind chimes an eerie signal to his departure.

"Don't bother," she muttered, dashing an angry hand across her eyes only to find the tears falling faster than before.

Furious at Cooper, furious at her useless tears, and

furious at her inability to see a clear way out of this mess, she marched into the kitchen and flicked on the kettle.

A cup of chamomile tea might not soothe her seething soul but it would go a long way to erasing the awful chill that had seeped into her bones at the thought she might lose this place.

And that Cooper didn't give a damn.

Chapter Twenty-Three

Cooper strode up Brunswick Street in desperate need of a caffeine fix, entering the first café at the end of the block, *The Red Rocket*.

Was there anything about this suburb that wasn't unique or designed to throw him into a spin?

From the minute he'd first set foot on this street he'd been slightly off-kilter and out of his depth, both foreign feelings that didn't sit well with him. He liked control, order, planning, and forward thinking. Instead, since he'd set his sights on acquiring Ariel's gallery, nothing had gone according to plan, particularly the conscience he'd suddenly grown.

The same conscience that now screamed he'd let Ariel down somehow, that he'd driven an irreversible wedge between them.

It hadn't been intentional. The proposal was business and he'd hoped that once the deal was behind them, she might be interested in catching up on a social level again.

Fat chance.

THE CHARMER

He could handle her teasing, her loaded barbs, and her occasional put down, but tears? No way.

The sound of her choked up voice and the glistening moisture on her cheeks had kicked him in the gut and sent him running out of the gallery, torn between wanting to comfort her and strangle her for making this deal more complicated than it had to be.

"What will you have?"

Cooper tried not to stare at the young guy taking his order but it was hard not to considering he sported enough metal studded through his face to construct a bridge and had a white stripe through his gothic black hair.

"Strong espresso, please."

"No worries. Coming right up."

He watched the guy saunter away, slashes in his denim jeans, a less-than-white cloth hanging out of his back pocket, and a black T-shirt featuring the café's logo, feeling way older than his thirty years.

He'd never considered himself overly conservative but spending time in this suburb made him feel ancient. Though this place wasn't too bad in the displacement stakes: brown vinyl booths, chrome modern chairs, plain wooden tables. The only eye-catching things in the café were the fire engine red menus and the metal-favouring staff.

"Here you go."

The waiter returned in record time and placed a tall, steaming espresso in front of Cooper. He inhaled, needing a jolt of caffeine steam to hot-wire his brain into coming up with a solution to the Ariel problem.

"Thanks," Cooper said, stirring two sugars into his coffee for added oomph and wondering why the waiter hadn't moved. "Is there something else?"

The waiter appeared nervous, the metal rod in his nose twitching. "Actually, there is. You look like a guy who'd appreciate art. Here, take a look at this."

He pulled a flyer from his back pocket—the opposite pocket to the one containing the dirty rag, thank goodness, and slapped it on the table. "This artist is awesome. She's having her first showing tomorrow and you should go. Tell all your friends."

Cooper glanced at the flyer as he took his first, welcome sip of coffee, almost snorting it out when he saw where the exhibition would be held.

'*Colour by Dreams, featuring Chelsea Lynch*'.

The artist's name rang a bell but he couldn't quite place it immediately.

"It would be cool if you brought a heap of people. The artist really needs support."

"And who are you? Her PR manager?"

Cooper admired the young guy's push, wondering if he was a friend of Ariel's rather than the artist. It wouldn't surprise him in the least if she had a whole string of guys like this ready to promote and support her.

Look how she had him feeling.

The guy grinned, sheepish. "No, I'm Monty, her boyfriend. Chelsea is the best and I said I'd help her out by passing out some flyers to customers. Hope you don't mind?"

"After you brought me a coffee this good? No problem."

"You're cool for a business dude," Monty said, giving him some weird hand sign involving his index and little fingers pointing up with the rest of his fingers down, before slouching away to try his sales pitch on the next customer.

Cooper picked up the flyer and studied Chelsea Lynch's short bio: local girl who had grown up in Fitzroy, won a scholarship to study art, first showing sponsored by *Colour by Dreams*.

The last fact interested Cooper more than the rest. Why would Ariel sponsor another artist? Weren't gallery showings as rare as the last piece of prime developing land in this street?

From what he'd read, it took most artists years of hard slog and self promotion to obtain a showing, yet here was a young artist starting out being sponsored by a gallery?

Cooper drained the rest of his coffee, folded the flyer, and tucked it into his jacket pocket, hoping the old adage 'out of sight, out of mind' might work. For some inexplicable reason, he felt like a big, bad bully for pushing the gallery deal and in the process, ruining the dreams of people like this new artist.

Not to mention ruining the dreams of another artist.

He had his own agendas, his own goals, but what if Ariel's dreams were just as important as his?

This is business...

No matter how many times he told himself it was only business, seeing Ariel's vulnerability had delivered a kick in the guts to his cool, aloof act he'd donned for the presentation.

She'd found a chink in his impenetrable armour and he didn't like it. Business was one thing, caring about the opposition another, and unfortunately, he'd grown to like the fiery artist with the zany dress sense.

Enough to forfeit your dream?

Shaking his head and wishing for a clear-cut solution to this new problematic development in his quest for success, he left payment for the coffee along with a hefty tip and headed for the door.

He didn't make it.

Ariel burst through the door and made a bee-line straight for him, and by her murderous expression it looked like her tears were a thing of the past and she'd rather skewer someone's head.

His.

Chapter Twenty-Four

"Tell me more about that lease business you mentioned earlier," Ariel said, resisting the urge to poke Cooper in the chest as she slid into the booth opposite the chair he'd just vacated. She preferred the soft, comfy vinyl to the hard backed chairs. Not that his choice surprised her: hard chair for a hard-ass.

"Would you like a drink?" He sat opposite her with obvious reluctance. "And how did you find me? Is stalking another of your hidden talents?"

Ariel toyed with the cutlery in front of her, particularly the knife, and contemplated all sorts of delightful ways she could use it on the infuriating man in front of her.

"Everyone in the street knows me and when I asked if they'd seen a tall, uptight guy in a fancy suit, the old man from the Nepalese shop pointed me straight here." She smirked, as he frowned at her uptight dig. "And no thanks, I don't want a drink, I want answers."

To give him credit, Cooper's sombre expression didn't change. Most guys would've called her out for her outrageous behaviour—from sniffling tears to cocky demands in less than ten minutes—but he took it in his stride, leaning back in his chair and folding his arms, his blue-eyed gaze unwavering.

"All the answers are in the proposal you asked me to leave with you."

"I'd rather hear about it from you. Besides, I don't have time to read a lot of legalese that you've probably peppered through that doorstopper of a document you prepared."

She sounded ruder by the second but she couldn't help it. Nerves brought out her worst: defensive, obnoxious, and pushy. Having her home and livelihood potentially ripped away did that to a person.

His eyebrow arched at her snark. "You could've heard more if you hadn't booted me out of the gallery."

She ignored the challenging gleam in his eyes and the tiny thrill that here was a guy she could match wits with, who gave as good as he got.

She glared. "Could've, should've, would've, but didn't. How about you tell me everything you know about that lease now?"

So she could run straight to the council offices and see if she had an easel to stand on.

He folded his arms, a casual gesture of a confident guy rather than a defence mechanism, and met her stare straight on.

"The council has had a ninety-nine year lease on the land twice. The original owners, when the land was pastoral, leased it to the council who later bought the lease once the owners offered it to them for a hefty price. As I told you before, your Barb signed a twenty-five year lease with the council, which was extremely generous, and that's up for renewal. I've spoken to several people within council who are ready to negotiate a

THE CHARMER

sale for the right price. If that happens, you get nothing, which is why it's in your best interests to vacate now, take what's on offer, and lease elsewhere. That about cover it?"

Ariel listened to every damning word, her heart sinking lower than Cooper's lousy offer. Could he be right about the council selling or was he toying with her like he had from the start?

Only one way to find out. Push him.

"The council won't sell." Her eyes narrowed, trying to get a read on him and failing, damn his impenetrable facade. "You're bluffing."

He leaned forward and rested his forearms on the table, drawing her attention to his long fingers that she'd noticed when painting him. Long fingers she'd fantasised about, skimming her body, bringing her pleasure…

"I'm not bluffing and I'd hate for you to find that out the hard way."

She wound a curl around her finger, meeting his unflinching stare while her insides quaked. He had to be wrong. She couldn't contemplate any other option. She'd made a promise to Barb, had a legend to upkeep, to continue the work Barb had started in the local community, and she couldn't let a guy like Cooper railroad her into making a decision out of fear.

"You've seen enough of this street to know the type of image the council wants to portray and the gallery is a vital part of the local colour," she said, sounding surprisingly calm while dread churned her stomach. "Besides, we do a lot to foster local talent, not to mention helping the street kids in the area."

"Street kids? What's your involvement with them?"

If his upper class lip had curled in derision, she

wouldn't have been surprised. His incredulous tone said it all.

Heat surged into her cheeks, a potent combination of anger and resentment that a guy like him wouldn't understand the first thing about what it was like to be starving, cold, and desperate, and that he'd dare question her about it.

"Never mind, street kids aren't relevant to your *business proposal*, are they?"

By the sharp flare of awareness in his eyes, he registered her venom-loaded barb.

Shaking his head, he pushed back from the table. "This is getting us nowhere. I've answered your question about the lease, I've tried to lay out the offer as plainly as I can. The figures are in the document, so once you have a chance to think it over, I'm sure you'll make the right choice. I'll call by later to hear your decision."

"Don't bother."

She leaped to her feet as he stood, knowing she should shut up and get out before she said something she'd regret. But her defensive hackles were well and truly bristling and her thoughts transformed to words faster than she could stop them.

"I'm not interested in anything you have to offer, now or ever. I know you've been hanging around me, acting nice, doing the buddy-buddy thing to soften me up, but it hasn't worked, so you storm into the gallery today doing your intimidation act. Which, I hate to tell you, hasn't been successful either. So why don't you quit while you're behind and leave me alone?"

To her amazement, he laughed, a hollow sound devoid of amusement. "Does this mean you won't have dinner with me tonight so I can get your final answer?"

She clenched her hands, wondering if they were too far

THE CHARMER

apart for her to take a swing at his patrician nose, knowing she abhorred violence and would never do it, but it was nice to dream when a big-mouthed, big shot deserved it.

"It means I don't want to ever see you again."

She turned on her heel, hoping her worn flip-flips wouldn't send her sprawling and spoil her attempt at a dignified exit.

"That's going to be hard, considering I've been invited to Chelsea Lynch's showing tomorrow and I'm all for supporting new talent."

She stiffened as he brushed past her, waving a flyer in her face with a smug smile as he held open the door. She didn't respond. She couldn't, considering it took all her concentration to walk past the guy who, while he couldn't take no for an answer and it annoyed the heck out of her, stood up to her like no one ever had.

And a small part of her admired him for it.

She liked this guy. Against her better judgement, with every instinct screaming they were worlds apart, and he spelled trouble with a capital T, she liked him.

Considering she didn't want to see his smug face ever again, what would she do about it?

"Ariel, wait."

If she had half a brain, she would've ignored him and kept going. Instead, something in his tone, a softening, made her stop.

"What do you want now?"

He broached the short distance between them and took hold of her upper arms, the warmth of his palms against her skin meaning she couldn't have bolted if she tried. "Why did you follow me?"

"Because I'm insane," she muttered, wriggling to get free.

It wasn't his probing question that had her wanting to flee as much as his touch, his firm hands scorching her with his particular brand of heat. The type of heat that made her lose her mind. Her arms tingling wasn't enough. She wanted that heat to spread through her body, to have his hands all over her, exploring, caressing, stroking. Every last inch...

"You listened to me in there where you wouldn't back at the gallery. What changed your mind?"

Damn him for being so observant, so persistent.

She stopped wriggling, her glare ferocious. A lesser man would've backed down. Cooper didn't flinch. "Fine, you want to hear the truth? I always keep a promise. Simple as that. I felt bad for reneging on my part of the deal when you'd been pretty good about posing so I could finish the portrait. That's it. You happy?"

She expected him to smirk or tease her for being such a sap. Instead, his blue eyes blazed with tenderness and before she knew what was happening, he'd enveloped her in hug.

"I am now," he murmured, his hands sliding around her waist, moulding her to him, sending her pulse into overdrive and her belly into free-fall. "I'm not the enemy, you know."

"Says who?"

She tried to pull back but his arms tightened, pinning her against him, and while logic told her to make a run for it, desire flowed through her body and made her wish he'd drag her back to the gallery this second so they could have sex.

Maybe once they got rid of all their pent up tension, Ariel might be able to steel herself against Cooper once and for all?

THE CHARMER

Or maybe she was making lousy excuses for wanting to get naked with the hottest guy she'd ever known?

"I can prove it to you," he said, tilting her chin up to gaze into her eyes, his blue eyes boring into her with an intensity she couldn't fathom.

"Prove what?" She'd lost track of the conversation the second her mind put the two of them together naked.

"Prove I'm not the enemy."

"And how are you going to do that? By schmoozing me?"

"Don't tempt me." His gaze focussed on her lips and her breath hitched.

Her lips parted as his head descended, blocking out the brilliant sunshine streaming down on them and she held her breath, her hands splayed on his chest, craving the feel of bare skin rather than expensive cotton.

Her eyelids fluttered shut and she tilted her head a fraction, craving the touch of his lips more than she'd craved anything in her entire life.

"I'll call you," he said against the corner of her mouth, his lips brushing hers in the briefest of almost-there kisses before pulling away.

What the?

Her eyes snapped open and she reeled from the disappointment of not locking lips with the most infuriating guy she'd ever met.

He stepped away and she steadied, knowing if she swayed towards him he'd know how truly pathetic she was. One minute she was telling him to get lost, the next she was offering herself to him. Sheesh. The sooner she dated again, the better.

It had been way too long since she'd been held by a guy

let alone had sex. Her excuse for her irrational behaviour and she was sticking to it.

"Whatever," she said, brushing an errant curl out of her face, turning the gesture into a casual wave as he smiled before walking away.

However, there was nothing remotely casual about the blood pounding through her body or how much she wanted the guy who had the potential to ruin her.

Chapter Twenty-Five

"Why the glum face, *bella*?"

Ariel summoned a smile for Sofia, knowing it fell short of her usual grin when the woman's dark eyes filled with concern.

"My muse is being stubborn," Ariel said, fiddling with the dimmer switch on the gallery lights, wanting to get the ambience just right before opening the doors to the public in ten minutes for Chelsea's show.

Sofia tapped her upper lip with a manicured, crimson fingernail. "Are you sure it's just your muse being stubborn?"

"What do you mean?" Ariel stepped back and studied the vibrant oil landscape in front of her, pleased with the vivid colours dancing beneath a soft spotlight.

"Maybe that delicious man has you in a spin and you're holding out on him? *Santo cielo*, what a dish that one is." Sofia kissed her fingertips and waved them heavenward—holy sky indeed.

Ariel smiled, her first genuine smile since her confrontation with Cooper yesterday. "That kind of dish gives me indigestion so I'd rather not talk about him."

She should've known not to deny anything too vehemently with Sofia. It only served to inflame her curiosity.

"Ahh...a lover's quarrel, perhaps?" Sofia's eyes sparkled with intrigue. "All great love affairs need drama and I think you have this with your young man, no?"

"No. And he's not my young man."

Ariel moved onto her next task, making sure the cheese platters were arranged just right and interspersed with the exotic dips and crackers, wishing a small, traitorous part of her soul didn't wish he was.

"Life does not have to be so tough all the time. What will be will be." Concern laced Sofia's words but Ariel mentally disagreed.

Life was tough. Hers always had been and she didn't know any better. Losing the gallery would be yet another example of it. A sad, heart-breaking example, as she lost the one thing that symbolised hope to her: hope for a better life, hope that good things could come out of bad, hope that she could be the type of person Barb would've wanted her to be. The type of person she wanted to be: successful, proud and independent. Qualities guys like Cooper took for granted.

Well, she'd show him.

If she could rustle up a cool million or so, that is.

"If there is anything I can do to help..." Sofia trailed off, quirking a stencilled eyebrow while draping a plump arm across her shoulders.

"I'll be fine," Ariel said, submitting to a quick hug before shrugging out of Sofia's embrace, wondering if the lie sounded as hollow to Sofia as it did to her.

She wouldn't be fine, considering the council had confirmed her greatest fear this morning: they were selling the land the gallery stood on. Like most councils around Melbourne, they were strapped for cash and in desperate need of more schools and health care facilities, so selling off the last piece of prime real estate in Brunswick Street was a no-brainer.

Of course, they'd given her an option. Come up with the cash herself or lose the gallery.

Some option. For a person struggling to meet the monthly rent, they may as well have handed her an eviction notice.

"Hey, you guys. Do you think everything looks okay?" Chelsea bounded up to them, red hair gelled into fearsome spikes, a funky beige leather ensemble draping her lithe body.

Ariel pasted a smile on her face and shot Sofia a pointed look to change the subject. "Relax, Chelsea. Your paintings look great and this showing is going to be a hit."

Chelsea's confident grin waned. "What if no one turns up?"

"Do not worry, *bambina*. I have told the whole of Melbourne. Everyone will come." Sofia flung her arms wide and Chelsea straightened, her confidence restored.

Grateful for Sofia's reassurance, Ariel wished her problems could be solved as easily. "Chelsea, why don't you make sure the inventory list and red sale dots are in order while Sofia checks on the wine?"

While she scooted out the back to brace herself for Cooper's appearance. Surely he wouldn't attend? He'd probably been trying to intimidate her yet again by saying he'd come to Chelsea's showing, wanting to up the pressure, turn the screws a little tighter.

Well, she had news for him. If he did show his sorry face here tonight, she'd be the only one doing any screwing over. She'd thought long and hard about her options all afternoon while preparing the gallery and as much as Cooper's offer seemed her only chance at getting a fresh start elsewhere, she couldn't do it. Taking his money would be selling out on her dream, selling out on her promise to Barb, and she wouldn't let that happen. She couldn't.

She would fight this with every weapon in her limited arsenal. She planned on approaching the National Trust, the Arts Council, the Victorian Grants Committee. Whatever it took, she would do it.

People depended on her, people like Chelsea who would never have a chance at discovery if it wasn't for the gallery, Barb's legacy, and as Ariel watched the young woman flit around the gallery one last time to ensure everything was in order, she knew there was no other choice.

She could never sell out and if Cooper or the local council wanted this piece of land, they would have to drag her screaming from it after she'd exhausted every avenue.

"Ariel, there's a crowd outside." Chelsea's hushed tone alerted Ariel to just how nervous the young woman was, because Chelsea never spoke in anything below a dull roar. "Shall I open the door?"

"Go ahead. It's your moment to shine." Ariel gave Chelsea's arm a reassuring squeeze, fervently hoping this wouldn't be the girl's first and last showing at *Colour by Dreams*.

Chapter Twenty-Six

He came.

Ariel knew the exact moment Cooper set foot in the gallery because the hair on the nape of her neck snapped to attention, as did most of the women in the room.

To give her credit, she averted her gaze after the first soul-wrenching moment when their eyes met and what could only be described as sizzling heat arced between them across the room.

But that one, loaded moment was all it took for her to imprint his powerful image on her brain: black jeans, black T-shirt, black leather jacket, the bad-boy wardrobe looking way too good on the uptight corporate shark.

Throw in the cocky grin, the sardonic glint in his too-blue eyes, and a natural confidence that turned heads, and she knew she'd have trouble getting through the rest of the evening.

He could've played fair and avoided her.

Since when did a guy like him, used to getting whatever he wanted in life, play fair?

"You can run but you can't hide," Cooper said, sneaking up on her in the studio kitchenette while she hunted for extra plastic cups under the sink.

Ariel's head snapped up and she avoided clunking her head on the rusty metal sink by an inch.

"Nice view, by the way."

With heat flushing her cheeks, she wriggled backwards from her awkward position and hoped her butt didn't look big in the crushed velvet hot pants, before mentally slapping herself for caring.

"What are you doing here? I told you not to come."

He leaned against the doorjamb and grinned, sending her pulse hammering. "In answer to your first question, I'm here because I'm interested in art. As for you telling me not to come, surely you know that I love a challenge?"

She clenched the bag of cheap plastic cups in her hand so hard they crackled. "That's what I am to you, isn't it? A challenge. *Let's see how much I can suck up to the flighty artist and watch her capitulate and hand me her gallery on a platter.* Well, I've got news for you, bozo. It isn't going to happen."

She expected him to frown, to glower, to muster that stern business expression like yesterday when he'd presented his lousy pitch. Instead, his infuriating grin widened.

"You're stunning when you're angry."

A tiny thrill of happiness shot through her—a girl had her pride, after all—before she fixed him with a glare designed to intimidate. "And you're full of it. Now, if you don't mind, I have to get back out there."

"Oh, but I do mind," he murmured as she attempted to push past him and, short of plastering her body against his in the doorway, she stopped and waited for him to lower his arm.

He did.

Only as far as her waist.

"You can keep running from me all night but I'm not going anywhere. We need to talk and I'm not leaving until that happens."

He soft words dripped with gentle persuasion but she barely registered them as the light touch of his hand resting on her waist sent her hormones into a tailspin. The warmth from his palm scorched through the snug velvet hugging her waist, branding her skin and enticing her to do all sorts of crazy things, like slide into his arms for an all-over body experience of that seductive warmth.

Stupid. She knew his touch didn't mean a thing. She knew flirting was second nature to a successful guy like him. And she knew, without a shadow of a doubt, that she should boot his butt out the door so quickly he wouldn't have time to register it.

Instead, she tilted her chin up, looked him straight in the eye, and said, "If you're sticking around, make yourself useful. I could do with a spare pair of hands."

With that, she plucked his hand off her waist, holding it a fraction too long before dropping it and walking away without a backward glance.

Chapter Twenty-Seven

"What a night." Ariel flopped onto a sofa, toed off her three-inch cork wedges, and rubbed her aching feet, wishing a cup of tea would miraculously appear in her hand.

"Would you like something to drink? A nice hot cup of tea perhaps?" Cooper squatted in front of her, still looking perky and gorgeous while she felt like a washed out rag.

"I knew I let you stay for a reason," she said, hating how her heart lurched at the tender expression on his face, at the way his lips curved in a smile, at the way he read her mind and knew exactly what she needed at that precise moment. "A cup of blackcurrant and apple tea would be great."

He grimaced. "That combo belongs in a kid's fruit drink."

"It's delicious. Then again, a caffeine addict like you wouldn't have a clue." She softened her dig with a smile and his answering grin warmed her from the inside out, better than a cup of tea.

"You sit tight and this clueless coffee connoisseur will bring your fruity concoction in a jiffy."

THE CHARMER

As Cooper straightened and strode away, she admired how the black denim moulded his butt and his long, lean legs. Predictably, her pulse raced and heat stole through her.

She shouldn't have let him stay.

She should've booted him out with the rest of the stragglers—an exuberant Chelsea and matchmaking Sofia—but she didn't have the energy. Besides, there was nothing he could say that would change her mind about selling the gallery and she wanted to make that clear.

Once she outlined her plans for raising the necessary funds, she had no doubt she'd see the back of Cooper Vance.

She should be rapt. Instead, an empty feeling blossomed in the vicinity of her heart and spread outward, icy tentacles of loneliness creeping through her and making her wish for all sorts of futile things.

She wished Cooper wasn't a callous businessman.

She wished they'd met under different circumstances.

Scariest of all, she wished she didn't have a huge crush on a guy who had no interest in her other than as a means to an end.

"Here we are, one cup of hot fruit punch as requested." He pretended to gag. "Gross."

Cooper handed her a steaming cup of tea and she inhaled the irresistible fruity aroma, sighing with pleasure after her first sip.

"Thanks. This is heaven," she said, tucking her feet under her and taking blissful sips while studying Cooper over the rim of her cup.

"You're easily pleased if that's your idea of heaven," he said, taking a seat next to her on the sofa, his proximity setting off warning bells in her head.

She could've scuttled away like a frightened mouse but

lethargy infused her body. She simply didn't have the energy to move, or the inclination, if she were completely honest. What did she expect to happen anyway? For the guy to kiss her senseless?

You wish.

The stupid thing was, she did, and she took several gulps of hot tea to ease the sudden tightness in her throat.

"You're not having anything?"

He shook his head. "I'm fine. Are you?"

Before she could decipher what he meant, he reached across the short space separating them and skimmed his fingertips across her cheek. "You look worn out. And as gorgeous as you are without makeup, I've never seen you with dark smudges under your eyes."

"I haven't been sleeping well," she muttered, glaring at the main cause of her insomnia and wishing he'd revert to uncaring business mode.

She could handle that guy. This softer, astute version of Cooper had the power to undo her in a second.

"I'm guessing that's partly my fault, huh?"

"There's no partly about it. It's all your fault."

His eyes widened and for a confusing second, guilt flickered in his gaze, like he didn't want to kick her out from the only home she'd ever known. But that couldn't be right. He'd outlined in clear terms why she needed to sell to him, but the longer he stared at her with concern, the harder it was to stay resentful.

"Having you breathing down my neck, trying to oust me from this place hasn't been pleasant," she said, focussing on the business side of things in the hope he wouldn't delve deeper and realise there was more to her sleepless nights than worrying about the gallery's future. "It's stressful, and you're talking to a person who doesn't do stress. Yoga, yeah. Meditation, yeah. Stress, no."

He pulled away from her, a tiny frown indenting his brow. "It doesn't have to be stressful if you'd listen to reason."

Anger shot through her and she placed her near empty cup on the floor. "Reason being?"

"I'm not going to rehash old ground," he said, leaning back in his corner of the sofa and spreading his arms across the top, looking way too confident. "You know my offer is fair, considering the council can kick you out of here once the lease is up and you'll be left with nothing."

"How about I kick you out of here right now?" She leaned closer, refraining from jabbing him in the chest at the last second. "Or better yet, you finally get the message that I'm not interested in anything you have to offer, ever, and walk on out of here of your own accord?"

"You're lying." His eyes darkened to midnight as he sat forward and lowered his arms. "I think you're very interested in what I have to offer."

Her heart thudded at his loaded response, at his nearness. He smelt so good, an intoxicating blend of sandalwood and something lighter that evoked a powerful response in her. She loved scents: fresh flowers, aromatherapy oils, rain on freshly cut grass, but none of her favourite smells came close to Cooper's heady scent.

Damn him, he knew how he affected her and he was rubbing her nose in it.

She'd show him.

"You're delusional." She waved her hand as if shooing a fly. "And if you're trying to imply there's something behind our occasional flirting, forget it. We both know you're slumming it for a while, getting to know how the other half live."

His jaw clenched, his eyes narrowed, and tension radiated off him in palpable waves. She moved in for the kill. If what she said next didn't get him out of her life once and for all, nothing would.

"Don't worry, I'm a big girl, I can take it. You spend time with the eccentric artist, flirt a little, soften her up, get her to buy into your crazy scheme. I get it. It's the way you do business. Take no prisoners, tell no lies, and all that crap." She shrugged, pretending like she didn't care, while her chest tightened with regret. "Hey, no hard feelings."

Though he'd been right to accuse her of lying. At least about the feelings part. She had feelings and plenty of them. Sadly, she couldn't do anything about them. Her life was complicated enough without letting her erratic emotions join the party.

"Are you finished?" He said, his tone low, menacing.

"Actually, I haven't. I also think you're snobby, condescending, cocky, and—"

His lips crushed hers into silence and she gasped in shock, realising a second too late that opening her mouth might be construed as an invitation.

Cooper didn't hesitate, deepening the kiss, challenging her to meet him half way, coercing her with a skilful precision that took her breath away.

He wasn't the only one who liked a challenge and in the split second where reason warred with passion, she threw caution to the wind and showed him exactly who he was messing with.

Her lips clung to his, frantic, desperate, meshing in a whirlpool of hot sensation that lit a fire deep within.

Her hands took on a life of their own, skimming the wall of his rock-hard chest before sliding higher, tangling in his hair to pull his head closer, to anchor herself in a world tilting crazily out of control.

Heat streaked through her body and she leaned into him, wanting more, needing more, and as his arms slid around her, hauling her across his body to lie on top of him, logic fled; to be replaced by a deep-seated yearning that this should go on forever.

"Wow," Cooper murmured, breaking the kiss to stare into her eyes, his hands pushing the curls off her face in a gentle caress.

She couldn't fathom his bewildered expression and reality hit as he shifted slightly beneath her. Here she was, lying on top of an extremely hot guy, a guy she could easily fall for in the blink of an eye if she completely lost her mind, a guy she'd been in the process of vanquishing from her life a few moments ago, a guy who had just sent her spiralling out of control with a simple kiss.

What the hell was she doing?

Maybe the kiss hadn't been simple. It had been downright amazing, but that wasn't the point. She still needed to get rid of him, and fast. No telling what her kick-started hormones might do in the next ten seconds.

She disengaged his hands from her face and slid onto the floor in an undignified heap before leaping to her feet like some bumbling clown act in a circus. "That was an interesting diversion but I hate to tell you, it didn't work. I still want you to get out of here."

Cooper stood with a lot more grace than she had, his inscrutable expression annoying her. Couldn't the guy at least look the teensiest bit shaken by the cataclysmic kiss they'd shared?

Then again, maybe it wasn't so extraordinary for him. He probably went around kissing half the female population in Melbourne like that. And no, that sharp stab of pain in the vicinity of her heart wasn't jealousy; it had to be all the cheese she'd consumed earlier mixing with the tea to give her heartburn.

"If you don't shut up, I'm going to kiss you again until you do."

She opened her mouth with an instant rebuke but shut it quickly as he took a step towards her. Then again, the thought of more of that sensational kissing wasn't so bad...

"Good, now that I've got your attention, I want you to listen. Yes, I want this deal to go through, and yes, it's very important to me. In fact, it's more than important, it's imperative."

He paused for a moment as if searching for the right words and she waited, prepared to give him a little leeway. After all, it's the least she could do before she planted her foot on his butt and booted him out the door permanently.

"As for what's happening between you and me, it's got nothing to do with business. Do I wish you were some shrivelled up old prune that wouldn't tempt me? Yes. Do I wish I could separate business from everything about you that entices me? Yes. Do I wish I could seal this deal and not look back without remembering the curve of your smile, the fire in your eyes, the passion of your kiss? You bet."

He shook his head as if trying to clear it, but confusion clouded his eyes. "But there's no use wishing for the impossible, and right now, pretending something doesn't exist between us would be doing just that and I won't. I can't."

Ariel gaped as she absorbed what Cooper had said while he stared her down, the bad-boy businessman daring her to disagree.

She couldn't help admire that he was man enough to acknowledge the spark between them. It didn't mean she had to agree with him or encourage him, despite how her heart raced at the wonderful things he'd said about her and that he found her just as attractive as she found him.

He was still the enemy and would tear her world apart given half a chance.

A chance she had no intention of giving him.

"Got nothing to say? Come on, give it your best shot," he said, the grim glint in his eyes at odds with his sardonic smirk.

"What do you want me to say?"

Apart from the obvious: *I like you, I desire you, I can easily lose my head and go crazy for you.*

But she wasn't the type of girl to lose her head. She had too much at stake, too many responsibilities, starting with making the gallery a viable proposition for the next umpteenth years as Barb would've wanted.

"How about you start with the truth?"

Ariel compressed her lips, a simple defensive gesture to prevent her from blurting a host of truths Cooper wouldn't want to hear: how the couldn't quell the relentless fear that the gallery would slip through her fingers despite how hard she worked to keep it afloat, the guilt that she'd let everyone down, and the biggie of them all, how out of depth he made her feel.

So, despite her penchant for brutal honesty, she opted for the easy way out.

She lied.

"There isn't anything between us beyond the usual guy-girl chemistry. We're opposites in every way and you want something from me I can't give you, *imperative* or not."

Avoiding his penetrating stare, she continued. "I won't sell, you don't get what you want, and we have no reason to keep meeting like this. So let's call it quits while we're both still being civil to each other, okay?"

She expected him to bamboozle her with more convoluted arguments, similar to the ones in his long-winded business proposal, to change her mind. She expected him to pressure her, to ram home the reasons why obtaining her gallery was imperative to him.

Instead, he surprised her again. He took a step forward, invading her personal space with his overpowering presence, and she resisted the urge to lean into him, to experience the thrill of having his arms slide around her one last time and make her forget every single reason why they couldn't be together.

He placed a finger under her chin, gently tipping it up, and stared into her eyes. "You know the interesting thing about chemistry? It can lead to explosive reactions and unexpected outcomes."

She should look away.

She wanted to look away.

Instead, she stared at him like a hypnotised dummy while his thumb brushed her bottom lip with infinite tenderness and he smiled, a hot loaded smile rather than the smug smile of a guy who knew how he made her resistance melt.

"And one more thing," he said. "Chemistry was my best subject at school and I love combining elements to create combustion."

Before she could gather her wits and tell him exactly what he could do with his elements, he hauled her into his arms and kissed her with the force of a man hell-bent on proving how great he was at chemistry.

This was her last chance. Push him away, ignore all the

great things he'd said about her, and forget that she hadn't had sex in three years.

Three long years.

He deepened the kiss, his hands winding through her curls, angling her head for better access, and the second his tongue touched hers, she lost it.

The point of no return.

She practically leaped on him, pushing him back against the sofa, her hands everywhere, sliding under black cotton, stroking the hot skin of his tight abs beneath.

Someone moaned, a low, sexy sound, and in the passionate haze that had invaded her brain, she had no idea if it was him or her. She didn't care. The scent of him, the feel of him, the taste of him, the sounds of ragged breathing and low moans set a spark to her latent libido and sent it up in flames in a raging inferno that promised to consume them.

"You sure about this?" Cooper broke the kiss for a second, capturing her face in his hands, staring deep into her eyes.

"Shut up and kiss me," she said, the blatant lust radiating from his too-blue gaze setting fire to any tiny residual doubt she may have harboured and sending it up in smoke.

"Your call, sweetheart."

And he did exactly as she'd instructed, with one heck of a difference.

He didn't hold back.

Their mouths clashed in a heated frenzy of lips and tongue, challenging, duelling, an erotic game where there were no losers, only winners.

Ariel sighed as his lips slid down her throat and she arched against him, bringing her into direct contact with his hard-on, his very impressive hard-on if the size of him against her belly was any indication.

"You're beautiful," he said, his lips ceasing their leisurely exploration as he swiftly unbuttoned her top and peeled it open, the anticipatory gleam in his eyes that of a guy opening the best present ever.

The few times she'd had sex in the past, she'd hated the undressing part. Plagued by inadequacies growing up, they manifested at the oddest of times, like now, when she hoped her boobs weren't a disappointment and he wouldn't find her too skinny.

"Stunning," he murmured, unclipping her bra with a deft flick of his fingers and staring at her breasts as if he'd found treasure, before capturing a nipple in his mouth.

"That feels so good." She writhed beneath him, burning up from the inside, wishing their clothes would disappear.

"You feel so good."

He set about proving it, drawing his tongue slowly across her chest, sucking one nipple then the other, feasting on her like he hadn't eaten in a decade.

Ariel throbbed in so many places she didn't know whether she should shock the living daylights out of Cooper and devour him now or prolong the sweet agony and let him continue to lavish her with more of the exquisite licking and sucking that was sending her into meltdown.

"I need you," she whispered, proving how much by sliding a hand between them and cupping his cock.

Cooper tensed, muttered a very sexy curse that she had every intention of doing to him, and pulled away, his stare so searing that desire shot through her veins, her nipples pebbled, and a heaviness settled in her core.

"I need you *now*."

He hovered over her, a sexy smile playing around his

mouth. "You know you're bossy and sassy and thoroughly irresistible, don't you?"

"I'll show you bossy."

She surged upwards, her hands against his chest, pushing him upright against the back of the sofa so she could straddle him.

He laughed, a low, wicked sound that provoked her to show him just how bossy she could be.

She whipped his T-shirt over his head in a second, before leaning forward to nuzzle his neck and drape her hair across his bare chest. He groaned and she smiled, a self-satisfied smile of a woman who knew she had the power to drive a guy crazy.

"Think you're in charge, huh?" His hands spanned her waist, holding her in place while he shifted beneath her, leaving her in little doubt that the second their clothes vanished, she'd be in heaven.

"You ain't seen nothing yet," she said, sliding off him to kneel at his feet, her fingers making short work of his zipper and button, easing the denim down his long legs with her gaze locked on his the entire time.

His low moan turned her on.

His glazed look empowered her.

His hard-on beneath tight black boxers encouraged her to toy with the elastic, brush her fingertips against his penis, and slowly, tantalisingly, peel the cotton down his legs.

"Oh wow," she said, sitting on her heels and admiring the view as liquid heat pooled between her legs. With reverence, she reached out to stroke him, to touch him.

At last.

Chapter Twenty-Eight

"Hell, Ariel," Cooper gritted out, hanging onto what little self control he had left when her hand wrapped around his shaft and started moving up and down in slow, rhythmic movements.

"Don't you mean heaven?" Her sassy mouth curved into a knowing grin as she flicked her thumb over the hood of his cock, sending him into overdrive.

"You're such a turn on." He stilled her hand, sliding to the floor next to her, grateful for the soft, plush rug over the wooden floorboards.

"Hey, what happened to me being in charge?"

"My turn," he said, knowing he couldn't last much longer.

He'd been fantasising about Ariel for too long, wondering what she'd look like naked, wondering what colour her nipples would be, wondering how she'd sound when he thrust into her repeatedly.

Her breasts were gorgeous, a perfect handful, with dusky pink nipples that hardened at the slightest provocation. Considering his hands and mouth hadn't left them alone since he'd taken off her top, they were very provoked.

He had to see the rest of her, taste the rest of her, feel her hot and tight around him before he lost it completely.

He slid a slow, sensual kiss across her swollen lips as he tugged at those sexy little hot-pants, pulling them off her in one, smooth tug. Thankfully, the red satin thong beneath got tangled up at the same time and when he broke the kiss to stare down at her, his sigh bordered on adoration.

"Yeah, yeah, I know. I'm a natural blonde," Ariel said, her nervous laugh cueing him in that getting naked with a guy wasn't the norm for her.

"You're stunning. Every exquisite inch."

He kissed her again, softly this time, teasing, pleasing, as his fingers delved, finding her clitoris and circling it with his thumb, loving the small, excited sounds she made in his mouth.

She broke the kiss and moaned, her head falling back, her breathing ragged as he slid two fingers inside her, his thumb stroking her folds, her clitoris, with increasing pressure.

"Cooper, that feels so good. Oh yeah..."

Their gazes locked as she convulsed around his fingers, her body arching upwards, her orgasm heating the gold flecks in her eyes until they glowed amber.

He had to have her at that precise moment, with her soft and pliant and sated in his arms.

"More," she murmured, her demand tempered with a smug smile.

He stared at her sassy mouth, knowing a woman like Ariel would be a never-ending source of surprises and hoping he'd get an opportunity to discover them all. Though he wasn't a fool. This was sex and she'd probably withdraw from him in the morning.

Not if he had his way. This attraction had been simmering between them right from the very beginning and he had no intention of letting this be a one night stand.

Besides, he had a feeling sex with the stunning artist could become addictive—very addictive—and he didn't have too many vices.

"More, huh? There's no pleasing some women." He rolled his eyes and she slapped him playfully on the chest.

"I'm pleased all right. You, on the other hand, could do with a bit of pleasuring yourself?"

She sent a pointed look at his groin, her fingers closing around his cock, and he groaned.

"Hold that...thought," he said, fumbling through the back pocket of his jeans for his wallet, grabbing a condom, and ripping open the little blue foil packet while Ariel continued to stroke him, her sexy chuckle driving him as insane as her hand.

Ariel loved the silky hardness of Cooper's penis, loved how much she turned him on. She reluctantly released him, watching him slide the condom on, her insides constricting at the thought that she'd soon be sheathing him just as effectively.

"Hurry," she said, wondering when she'd become such a sex-starved floozy and not particularly caring.

She wanted Cooper. Inside her, pleasuring her, hard and hot and pounding, satisfying the ache that had begun the first time he'd taken his clothes off for her.

"Come here." Cooper opened his arms to her and Ariel didn't hesitate, straddling him, kissing him, revelling in the hard tip of his penis nudging at her entrance as she sunk down, almost passing out with sheer satisfaction as he stretched her, filled her.

"You feel...fucking amazing..." He groaned, loudly, as she raised up and sank down again, taking him in deeper, relaxing her muscles around him, savouring the fullness, the heat.

"Good?"

"Sensational."

She kind of lost it after that. He did too. Their sweat-slicked skin slid together, over and over, until the friction became unbearable.

All she could focus on was him. Caressing her. Stroking her. Filling her. Thrusting over and over until she was mindless with pleasure.

Her orgasm built quickly again and she didn't care. She wanted him. She wanted it all.

Her hands speared his hair and she bit into his shoulder as he thrust upwards so hard she almost hit the ceiling. She convulsed around him, her muscles clenching, savouring his hardness pounding into her softness, clawing at a release that promised to be cataclysmic.

Every nerve ending pinged and heat flushed her body as he flipped her over, driving into her with a wild abandon that sent them both into orbit.

Her primal yell mingled with his loud groan, and as she floated back to her senses, her first thought was 'that was absolutely incredible.'

Closely followed by 'what the hell have I done?'

Chapter Twenty-Nine

Pale gold filtered through the tiny bathroom window, heralding the dawn of another perfect Melbourne day.

Though it wasn't just another day.

Ariel braced herself on the antique washbasin, staring at her tousled reflection in the bevelled mirror.

You had sex with Cooper Vance.

And not just ordinary sex. Scintillating, mind-blowing, burn up the sheets sex, though they never quite made it to the bed until later. Much later.

She'd never be able to look at her favourite rug in the studio again without remembering the way he'd felt inside her, the way he'd touched her all over, the way he'd made her crave him with every turned on cell in her body.

The man was a menace.

She'd known it from the first second he set foot in her studio and now she had proof.

Closing her eyes, she leaned forward and rested her forehead against the cool glass.

What had she done?

THE CHARMER

She'd been doing her damnedest to push him away, to ignore the sizzling attraction between them, to focus on saving her business; and that meant getting as far from the corporate shark as possible.

Instead, she'd melted into a puddle of lust the minute he kissed her and nothing would ever be the same again.

At least, not for her.

She didn't do casual sex, never had. She could count her past encounters on one hand and each had been with guys she'd been dating for a while. The scary thing was, nothing about last night with Cooper felt casual. She felt like she *knew* him and that scared her more than the way she'd jumped him; or how much she'd enjoyed it.

"You okay?"

Ariel jerked upright and her eyes flew open, only to wish she'd kept them shut. The sight of Cooper behind her —naked Cooper—reflected all too clearly in the mirror and her heart flipped.

"Fine. Just a bit tired."

"I'm not surprised." His warm, intimate smile notched up the temperature in the bathroom by a hundred degrees.

"I didn't mean to wake you," she said, fiddling with the tie of her favourite kimono, wishing he'd stop staring at her like he was starving and she was breakfast. "I'm usually up pretty early."

"No problem."

An awkward, tense silence stretched between them she would've given anything to avoid. Why couldn't he stop gawking at her, get dressed, and get the hell out of her life?

She knew her jitters stemmed from the startling realisation how much he meant to her and the phenomenal sex only solidified it. So how could she extricate from this morning-after scenario without making a fool of herself?

His eyes met hers in the mirror and she glimpsed confusion. Join the club.

"You're okay about what happened last night, right?"

To her annoyance, she blushed. "Fine."

"You sure about that?"

She stiffened as he came closer and slid his arms around her waist from behind, leaving her no option but to lean back against him or jump up onto the antique vanity to avoid him.

"You're gorgeous," he murmured, nuzzling her neck, sending shivers through her body, resurrecting erotic memories of the way he'd kissed every inch of her last night. Every single tingling inch...

"And you're crazy," she said, grimacing at her reflection —frizzy hair, swollen lips that looked like they'd been ravaged all night, wide, luminous eyes filled with fear.

Fear of what happened next, fear of how much she'd miss Cooper once he exited her life, fear of never finding a guy to make her feel half as good as he'd made her feel last night.

"Whose fault is that?" He kissed his way up her neck, turning her around slowly, staring deep into her eyes. "You make me crazy. With your sexy smile, your incredible eyes, and that mouth that makes me want to do everything I did with you last night and so much more."

His compliments warmed her heart but she had to establish some distance between them before she did something stupid. Like drag him back to her bed and ensure they didn't leave it for the next forty-eight hours.

"You can cut the sweet talk. I'm a sure thing, remember?"

"Time for you to shut that sassy mouth of yours. Again," he said, lowering his lips to hers, and his slow, sensual kiss would've curled her toes if she hadn't been standing on them to reach him, desperate for one more taste of his lips but hating her treacherous body for it.

"I thought you said you didn't have any more condoms?" By the feel of his boner pressing against her stomach, she guessed he wasn't popping into the bathroom for a quick goodbye. More like a quickie something else.

"I don't." His hands strummed her back through the silk of her kimono, the steady strokes making her arch like a cat. Next she'd be purring. "Don't worry, we won't need them. I was only planning on taking a shower, that's it."

She didn't believe him, as he tugged on the knotted tie and peeled open the front of her kimono. He skimmed her skin, teasing with his touch, brushing her nipples with his thumbs until they peaked in sweet agony.

Her breath hitched as he slid the silk from her body with infinite patience, one exquisite inch at a time until the kimono pooled at their feet in a slash of vibrant emerald against the white tiles.

"I don't think my shower's big enough for the both of us," she said, eyeing the small glass cubicle, considering Cooper took up most of the bathroom already.

"All the better for a nice close fit."

With an arm firmly draped around her waist, he turned on the hot and cold taps with his other hand, tested the water temp, and took the opportunity to turn the five second wait into another scorching kiss.

She could've shrugged out of his grip.

She could've picked up her kimono and stalked from the bathroom with what little dignity she had left intact.

But where was the fun in that?

She'd spent a lifetime being serious—first surviving the foster system, and later being the model niece for Barb—and more recently, worrying about how to keep the gallery afloat. She never had time for fun. And that's what this last taste of Cooper would be: pure, unadulterated fun.

"You coming in?" He arched an eyebrow, his arm loosely draped around her waist. "The water's warm."

He waited, wearing nothing but a sexy, persuasive smile, as Ariel mentally recited every rational reason she shouldn't do this.

He's your enemy. This could be another ploy to soften you up. He's not your type. He's your opposite in every way. He'll break your heart.

Her conscience made a lot of sense, but she always listened to gut instinct and right now, she wanted one, last taste of Cooper.

With a coy glance from beneath her lashes, she said, "You bet," and stepped with him into the shower.

A staunch environmentalist, Ariel conserved water by taking short showers even though she loved the hot spray peppering her skin. Today, however, her ideals flew out the window along with her reservations as she leaned against Cooper, her back wedged against his front, while his hands travelled her body in long, slow strokes. Soaping, circling, teasing, turning her legs to jelly before he delved between them and brought her to a knee-buckling orgasm with a few deft flicks of his fingers.

"I can't stand up," she murmured, sinking against him further, joining in his chuckles when he clunked his head on the nozzle trying to support her.

"That's not funny." He rubbed his head and the harder he tried to frown, the more they laughed until she clung to him in mirth rather than desperation.

"You're a dangerous woman," he said, pulling her into a tight hug that squeezed the air out of her. Or was it the intensity in his blue-eyed stare that robbed her of the normal function of breathing?

"Not really." She winked. "But I can be."

He'd given her so much pleasure, time to return the favour.

Reaching between them, she captured his cock in her hand, stroking until he groaned, loving the ecstasy etched on his face as she slid up and down the shaft.

They watched as she picked up tempo, and she'd never felt so empowered as he came in a hot rush.

His head fell back, exposing the strong column of his neck, and Ariel placed a gentle kiss there, knowing they could never recapture this moment, shocked by how sad that made her feel.

As Cooper opened his eyes and smiled, before resting his forehead against hers, she couldn't say a word. As water sluiced down on them, she knew why.

They had nothing left to say.

After all, what can you say when you've just screwed the enemy?

Chapter Thirty

Cooper knew the precise time his revamped proposal had been delivered to Ariel: ten o'clock. Now, the timestamp on his computer read twenty-five and it would've taken her twenty-five minutes to high-tail it to *Vance Corporation* in Melbourne's CBD, including the time she would've spent jumping up and down on the spot having a tantrum.

She would hate the amendments he'd made to the proposal.

If the ruckus outside his office door was any indication, she intended on making her feelings known to all and sundry before she even made it into his office.

As he pushed back from his desk and strode across his office, the door flung open.

"You've got a nerve!" Ariel shouted, making a beeline for him while Beryl, his secretary, gave an apologetic shrug and made circles with her finger at her temple.

"I'll take it from here, thanks Beryl," he said, walking straight past Ariel to shut the door.

THE CHARMER

Not that it would make much difference. Half of Flinders Street would've heard Ariel's indignant shriek as she whirled and advanced on him, her eyes filled with emerald fire and her curls bristling like a fuzzy halo.

Not that there was anything remotely angelic about her, considering what they'd got up to last night and in the shower first thing this morning.

He couldn't get the images of their incredible night out of his head, which is exactly why he'd headed to the office after he left her gallery. He hated feeling off-kilter and that's how Ariel made him feel. Business grounded him and gave him a purpose. He needed clarity now more than ever and once this deal went through, he'd have it. Then he could re-evaluate his feelings for Ariel and what that meant for them.

"Why don't you take a seat and we can discuss the new developments like two rational adults?"

"Rational?" She drew back her shoulders, drawing his attention to her breasts straining against the paisley halter top that moulded her like a second skin, eliciting erotic memories of the way she'd felt lying on top of him last night—passionate, feverish, responsive—like a fantasy come to life. "You expect me to be rational when you have a courier deliver me *this*?"

She reached into a straw carryall, pulled out a sheaf of papers, flung them onto his desk, and planted her hands on hips, like an avenging demon come to slay him. "Tell me this isn't what it looks like."

"What does it look like?"

He shouldn't antagonise her further, he really shouldn't, but a small part of him was enjoying their confrontation. She'd had all the comebacks last night, shooting him down in flames when all he'd tried to do was lay the foundations for a possible future as friends or maybe something more.

She hadn't listened to him, she hadn't acknowledged his honesty, and she sure as hell hadn't given them a chance even after the mind-blowing sex. If he were completely honest with himself, he didn't know if he wanted a future with Ariel, but he'd be damned if he walked away without exploring the fireworks that exploded whenever they were within two feet of each other.

She continued to confuse business with pleasure and the only way he knew to bring this to quick closure was to finish the business and move onto more of the pleasure. A lot more...of her soft lips clinging to his, her hands all over his body, her excited little moans as he licked her to orgasm...

"What is wrong with you?" She broached the short distance between them and snapped her fingers in front of his face. "Cut the vague act and start explaining."

Wrestling his raging libido into some semblance of control, he headed for the safety of his desk and away from Ariel's intoxicating scent. He'd never smelt anything like it and the weird perfume he could now label as neroli thanks to the tiny essential oil vial he'd spied in her bag the other day had grown on him. He doubted he'd ever smell oranges again without remembering the blonde goddess with eyes of green fire.

"Would you like a drink?"

"No. I would like an explanation." She grudgingly sat on the leather chair opposite his and folded her arms like a recalcitrant schoolgirl waiting for punishment from the principal. "Now."

He sat, straightening the messy papers scattered on his desk, hoping a few extra seconds would help calm her down. When he caught her eye and saw the narrow green slits glowing with anger, he knew a few extra hours wouldn't help.

"If you've read the amendments, you don't need an explanation. It's clear."

"The part where you're threatening me or the part where you'll do anything to get your grubby hands on the gallery?" She leaned forward, her fingers clenching his desk so hard the knuckles whitened. "Oops, silly me. The gallery doesn't mean a thing to you, it's the land you're after. I really must learn to clarify my terms, like you have in this pathetic excuse for a proposal."

He let her vent. He'd expected the animosity, the antagonism, but it hurt nonetheless. He cared about her. And he hadn't realised how much until now, when she glared at him with loathing and contempt.

Damn it, what if his plan backfired?

What if, in attempting to finish the business side of things and move onto the personal, he finished them completely?

"I'm not threatening you, Ariel, I'm giving you an opportunity to come out of this deal a winner."

"You're trying to buy me off to get what you want." Her scornful stare burned a hole straight through to his conscience. "And if I don't comply, you go ahead and offer the council twice what the land is worth by the end of today?"

She shook her head, golden curls rioting around her face and a perfect contrast for the faint pink staining her cheeks. "Wow, lucky me, that's some *opportunity*."

He gritted his teeth, wishing it didn't have to be this way. "This deal has to go through. Today," he said, feeling like a heel when the fire drained from her eyes only to be replaced by fear.

"I need more time."

Her whispered plea slammed into his soul, raising questions he'd rather ignore.

Was his dream more important than hers?

Did he care enough about her to turn his back on the primary motivating factor that dragged him into the office these days, the thought of leaving and never coming back once he sealed this deal?

If he cared about her, how much? And what was he going to do about it?

"Time isn't going to help," he muttered.

It would help either of them. He needed to get out of *Vance Corporation*, she needed to start a new gallery elsewhere with the money he was determined she would have. And once this pesky business was out of the way, they needed to recreate the fire that had consumed them last night, repeatedly.

"You don't know that. There's the National Trust, the Victorian Arts Council..." she trailed off, the truth finally dawning in her stricken eyes. "You've already made the offer, haven't you?"

Cooper hesitated, knowing he couldn't lie to the woman he loved yet aware the truth would potentially ruin what little chance they had for a future.

The woman he loved?

He slumped in his chair, the truth detonating.

He loved her...

No way.

He must've slipped up under the strain, substituting the L word for caring. Yeah, that sounded better. He cared for her. Much better.

Yet when he met her defeated stare, unshed tears glistening green, his heart made a mockery of his head.

For a guy who thrived on cool, hard facts, who used logic to sort through problems, an emotion he had little time for had snuck up and sabotaged him.

The longer Ariel stared at him, the worse his heart ached, until it took every ounce of willpower not to leap from his chair and cradle her in his arms.

"Tell me the truth."

Cooper startled, shocked that she'd seen right through him in his moment of clarity, before realising she meant the truth about his offer to the council. Worse, that what he was about to say would rob him of any chance to express his newly discovered feelings to the woman who needed to hear him out.

Taking a deep breath, he selected his words carefully. "I have approached the council and had discussions about the sale of land, but nothing has been formalised."

"But you've basically thrown more money at them than they know what to do with, right? So if I don't accept your offer and sell before the lease is up, they're going to jump at it straight away?"

He nodded, hating the dejected slump of her shoulders, the shaking hand that fiddled with a curl near her right ear, winding it furiously around and around.

"So what was the extra time about? Giving me another twenty-four hours to stew before I finally capitulate and make your day?"

Scorn dripped from every word and she straightened, anger replacing defeat in her eyes.

That's my girl, he thought, admiring her fighting spirit yet wishing he wasn't the one to instigate it.

"I want you to do this of your own accord, to make the decision yourself."

She laughed, a harsh, hollow sound that had nothing to do with happiness. "That's rich, coming from you."

Tapping her temple, she looked heavenward as if deep in thought. "Let me see. I get to make my own decision as long as it's by the end of today and it's what you want. Thanks *sooo* much."

The hatred in her eyes cleaved his heart in two. "We're going round in circles here. That's my final offer and as a smart businesswoman, I think you should take it."

Though it wasn't his final offer, not if he had any say. Once this mess got sorted and they could put business behind them, he had a host of other offers in mind, the main one being a relationship.

He didn't have a lot of experience with love.

He'd loved his mum; she'd died when he was too young.

He loved his dad; Eric may as well have died for all the attention he'd paid Cooper since he joined the firm.

He learned love wasn't a reliable emotion but one thing was for certain, he loved Ariel, and he'd make damn sure he gave it his best shot.

Her steady gaze eyeballed him. "Why is this deal so important to you? You've used words like imperative to justify it yet I don't understand why a ruthless businessman like you would fluff around for a few weeks, posing almost naked, going out for coffees, attending art shows, when you could've shafted me right from the start. What's really going on?"

Cooper bit back an ironic smile. She'd given him a chance to hint at his burgeoning feelings.

And get the same reaction he had last night before they'd had sensational sex and he'd revealed how much he liked her? No way. Making a total ass of himself twice in less than twenty-four hours wasn't his style.

He settled for semi-truth. The least he could do considering she'd stood up to everything he'd thrown at her and then some.

"This deal is my ticket out of here. It's something I've been planning for a while now and I really need to make it happen."

Her lips twisted in a cynical smile. "Why? Aren't they paying you enough? Not enough perks? The boss got you over a barrel?" She snorted. "Though with a company name like *Vance Corporation*, I'm guessing you big shots keep it all in the family."

Ironic, considering he'd lost the remainder of his family —his dad—that fateful day a year ago when he'd signed on the dotted line, beyond excited to be working with someone of Eric's reputation. Back then, he had big dreams, the two of them working side by side and taking this company into the stratosphere.

Too bad his dreams had turned into nightmares.

"My father's the CEO," Cooper said, knowing how chuffed Eric would be about being labelled a big shot. That's all his father cared about these days: making money, acquiring prime land, developing properties. At the expense of the things that used to matter to him, like fishing, four wheel driving, and camping with his son.

Despite Cooper's drive to leave *Vance Corporation* behind, he knew he'd miss his dad. It was the only time they saw each other these days and as much as it hurt to be shut out of Eric's life, Cooper hadn't given up on him completely. Maybe his father would realise the cliche 'absence makes the heart grow fonder' held an element of truth and would make an effort to patch things up once Cooper left?

He hoped so, but he wouldn't hold his breath.

Ariel quirked an eyebrow, losing none of her sass despite the anger tightening her exquisite features. "So it can't be the pay or the perks that's the problem if daddy holds the purse strings. What is it? The executive bathroom not up to scratch? You've lost your car park?"

I've lost my best mate, my dad.

And it hurts like the devil.

He could've articulated his loss, but now wasn't the time. Not when she bristled like an angry echidna. He settled for "It's time for me to go it alone. You of all people should understand that."

Ariel blushed and squirmed in her seat, and he held up his hand to ward off whatever she was about to say when she opened her mouth.

"My motivation is irrelevant. What needs to be done right now is you placing your signature on the dotted line before five o'clock today. That's all that matters."

He rustled papers, hoping she got the message. He needed to concentrate on the business at hand and away from the sensitive topic of his motivation, because the momentary concern he'd glimpsed in her eyes had him wanting to blurt the sorry tale just to get it off his chest.

But he couldn't. He was a guy, a tough Aussie bloke, a man's man supposed to stifle his feelings and get on with things. His dad's mantra, not his. And for the last year, he thought his dad's mantra sucked.

"All that matters?" she muttered, grabbing her bag and leaping from her chair like she'd sat on hot coals. "What matters is that you're a selfish, spoiled rich boy who always gets what he wants. You don't care about who gets trampled on the way or whose dreams you ruin. And to think, I was actually feeling empathy for you a few seconds ago, about the going it alone doing it tough thing."

"I don't need your pity." He shot to his feet, torn between wanting to blurt the truth and telling her to get the hell out for her damning character assessment.

Though he didn't know what rankled more: that she thought so poorly of him or the tiny, niggle of truth in what she'd said.

He was selfish.

He did want this deal to go through, whatever the cost.

But what if it cost him the woman he loved?

"I guess not. A guy like you wouldn't need anything from a girl like me." She sneered. "Besides sex, of course, and now that you've got that, it's back to business as usual."

He'd been grateful she hadn't mentioned what had happened at her place last night, preferring to focus on their business discussion, separate from the other important issue: them. But now she'd mentioned it, they had another confrontation looming and he hoped the fallout wouldn't ruin them completely.

"That's not fair," he said. "We talked about what happened last night before I left this morning. Our relationship has nothing to do with this."

"You would say that."

Her scathing glare of condemnation kicked him in the guts before she headed for the door.

"Last night was incredible, Ariel and you know it. Don't spoil it by bringing business into it."

She hesitated at the door but didn't turn around.

Damn it, the sooner this deal went through, the sooner he could move onto more important things, like showing this stubborn, beautiful woman how much she meant to him.

"This needs to be finalised, Ariel. Today."

She ignored him and strutted out the door, slamming it in her wake, a hollow, empty sound that reverberated through his soul as he realised she'd slammed the door on any chance of a future between them.

Chapter Thirty-One

Eric barged into Cooper's office, shirt sleeves rolled up to the elbows, no tie, and a killer crease in his navy trousers, his usual work garb. His father never conformed, though he expected nothing less than perfection in his employees. "What's all the ruckus about?"

Cooper sank into his chair and gestured for his dad to take the seat Ariel had just vacated. "Ariel Wallace was here."

Cooper held up his hand to forestall his dad's usual interrogation. "The deal will be done by the close of business today."

"Good."

Cooper struggled to hide his surprise at his father's one syllable answer without a hint of emotion. He'd expected cartwheels from the man who had been after the last piece of prime land in Fitzroy since forever.

However, what shocked him more was his father' morose expression. It resembled how Eric had looked after his wife's funeral, the same devastating lost look that came with realising you would never see that person again, would never talk to that person again, share a hug or a laugh with them again.

"What's up? You don't sound so thrilled."

Cooper expected Eric to give him the brush-off, the usual 'back to business' gruff response he normally got.

Instead, his dad ran a hand through his thick thatch of peppery grey hair, his gaze darting around the room as if he wanted to look anywhere but at him. "Guess I can't change your mind about leaving?"

"No, Dad. You can't," Cooper said, deliberately keeping his voice devoid of emotion.

Close on the heels of his draining confrontation with Ariel—and the stunning realisation he loved her—he didn't need this. He'd waited long enough, hoping his dad would broach the yawning gap between them. He'd given his all to *Vance Corporation*, playing the dutiful son, trying to prove his worth rather than live off the family name, but it looked like his best efforts weren't good enough.

Nothing he could do or say would ever be good enough for his father and he'd stuck around too long already. Time to cut his losses and hope that his dad would realise what he'd lost when Cooper wasn't around every day.

"That's the first time you've called me Dad in a long time," Eric said, the uncertainty in his eyes surprising Cooper.

His dad was never uncertain about anything. Ruthless, domineering and pushy, yes. Uncertain and plagued by doubt? No way.

The crafty old devil. This had to be the old man's last ditch effort to make him stay at the company.

"I haven't called you Dad because you haven't encouraged familial bonds since I joined the company," Cooper said, opting for blunt honesty to get this over and done with.

THE CHARMER

No use rehashing the last year and how Eric had squandered his right to be called dad.

Once again, Eric surprised him. Rather than blustering his way out of an unwelcome topic and changing the subject, his dad seemed to crumple before his eyes: slumped shoulders, head slouched forward, mouth slack with pain.

"Forget I said anything—"

"No." His dad's head snapped up and some of the familiar fire blazed in his dark eyes. "You're right. I don't blame you for not calling me dad. I've been a prick, pushing you away. Not giving you the acknowledgement you deserve. Staying away from you." He shook his head. "I've made a mess of everything."

Cooper didn't respond, considering he agreed with everything his dad had just said. Besides, Eric had a look he hadn't seen in twelve months, a look that he genuinely cared about Cooper enough to want to talk to him about something other than business.

"I thought I'd never recover from losing your mother but having you got me through her death." He dragged a hand through his hair and it shook. "You were my world. Then you started working here..." Eric drifted off, pain glazing his eyes and accentuating the multitude of lines fanning out from their corners.

"But that's what you wanted," Cooper said, confusion lending a sharp edge to his words.

"I know." Eric raised pain-stricken eyes to his, his mouth twisted into a grimace. "Seeing you every day has been the only reason I've been able to function, to get up in the mornings and make it into the office."

"Then why?"

Cooper didn't have to add *'why ignore me? Why treat*

me like dirt? Why act like I didn't exist, like I wasn't your son anymore?'

"Because I'm a gutless old fool who saw his life flash before his eyes the minute you sealed your first deal." Eric dragged in a deep breath and blew it out again, embarrassment flushing his cheeks. "I'm jealous, Son. I've been so jealous I couldn't see straight. Throw in the fear I'll soon be redundant, and the fact you keep negotiating deals I can't seem to seal these days, and there you have it. The most pathetic old fool you'll ever see."

"You're *jealous*?" Stunned, Cooper pondered the revelation, knowing there had to be more to it. "That's it?"

His dad sagged before his eyes. "Age does stupid things to a man. I was bursting with pride when you first signed that contract to work at the company, then within two months, I wanted to boot your cocky ass out the door."

"Then why hold me to the contract? Why not let me go months ago when I wanted to?"

Eric looked away. "Because you're an asset to the company. You've brought more business in over the last year than I have in the last five years. I pushed you harder, knowing you wouldn't disappoint."

"You took advantage of the fact your son wouldn't tell you to shove it," Cooper said, glad he'd discovered the reason behind his dad's animosity but feeling like he was still missing a major piece of the puzzle.

"There's something else."

Cooper leaned forward, not sure if he'd heard Eric's whispered words.

"What?"

"A guilty conscience." Eric shook his head, sorrow ageing him. "*Masterson's* approached me just after you started here. They were headhunting you, heard about the whiz kid from uni, knew you were my son. They were fishing around, wanting to know if you'd signed a binding contract, that sort of thing." Eric grimaced. "All over a friendly beer, of course. They were going to approach you directly after paying me the courtesy visit, so I lied to put them off."

A light bulb went off in Cooper's head. "So that's why you made me sign a contract like everyone else the month after I started?"

Eric nodded, his mouth downturned. "I told them you were legally bound to *Vance Corporation* and that was that."

"Before I signed the contract?"

"Uh-huh."

"Was their offer any good?"

"Unbelievable." Eric hesitated, wringing his hands before continuing. "I'm sorry, Son. I was selfish, wanting you to carry on the family tradition. Then when I had you where I wanted you, I couldn't handle your success." He tapped his temple. "Stupid, irrational, call it what you like. I'm an idiot."

Cooper digested his father's revelations, knowing he should feel more angry, more deceived. Instead, a strange feeling of relief seeped through him. He finally knew the truth and his father's indifference and belligerence over the last year had been born of insecurity, not a lack of love, as Cooper had thought.

His dad might be a lying old coot and going a bit senile but now he knew everything, he had more important things to worry about: like convincing Ariel that he wasn't the bastard she thought.

"I know I've treated you like crap but I want you to know I'm damn proud of you, Coop."

Finally, his dad looked at him with pride, with recognition, with love, and Cooper smiled.

"For a smart guy, Dad, you've made some pretty dumb judgement calls, but I'm willing to forgive and forget if you'll do one thing."

"What's that?" His dad glared at him with some of his characteristic suspicion and Cooper's grin widened.

"Go fishing with me this weekend. Have a beer or two, just like old times."

"I'd like nothing better, Son."

Eric's grin matched his and Cooper wished they'd had this conversation months ago.

"Does this mean you're staying?" Eric asked.

"Don't push your luck, old man."

Though his dad had posed a valid question.

Today was the first time he'd really looked at his dad in a long time and Cooper didn't like the changes he'd missed over the last year because he'd done everything to avoid being in the same room as his father. His dad looked older, more fragile than he had in ages, and maybe now wasn't a great time to spread his wings and leave the Vance nest, particularly as it looked like re-establishing familial bonds would be high on both their priority lists for a while.

Eric held up both hands as if warding him off. "Fine, fine, no harm in trying. By the way, is there something going on between you and the Wallace woman?"

Cooper hesitated a second before answering. "No, why do you ask?"

Not a complete lie, considering Ariel would probably never speak to him again after today.

His dad shrugged. "Just a hunch, by the doomsday expression on your face when I first came in here, and by the tears streaming down her face as she raced out of your office after slamming the door."

"A difference of opinion," Cooper said, his heart stuttering at the thought of Ariel crying over what he'd done.

"Looked more like a lover's tiff than a difference of opinion over a business deal to me." His dad paused, giving him ample opportunity to deny it, but Cooper merely clamped his lips together. "Then again, what do I know? I'm a stupid old fool and now we both know it."

His dad rose to his feet, pushed his shirt sleeves higher, and stuck out his hand. "You know I'm proud of you, Son?"

"Thanks, Dad." He shook hands with his father, filled with hope for their future.

After Eric left the office, Cooper sank into his chair, the relief of reuniting with his father fading as he realised he had to come up with a way to rectify the monumental mistake he'd made with Ariel sooner rather than later.

Chapter Thirty-Two

Ariel dabbed her paintbrush in the crimson daub on her palette and slashed across the canvas propped on the easel in front of her.

Red, the colour of anger and fury.

She followed with a dab and slash of ebony.

Black, the colour of darkness and gloom.

Another slash, this time with sunshine yellow.

Yellow, the colour encapsulating that lily-livered, no-good, Cooper Vance, the coward.

She slashed at the canvas with her brush over and over, combining colours in a frightening free-for-all of rage and disappointment. The painting would never see the light of day but it soothed her battered soul nonetheless.

The colours summed up her mood perfectly. She'd never felt as angry, gloomy, or scared as she did right now, the afternoon she would lose her dream. Not to mention renege on a promise to Barb that she'd vowed to keep.

Cooper Vance was evil. He'd used her, schmoozing up to her, acting like a friend, playing on her emotions, initiating her into the best sex she'd ever had in her life, making her love him and all for what? To whip the gallery right out from under her nose anyway.

What Cooper wanted, Cooper got, and she'd been justified in calling him a selfish spoiled brat earlier. She just wished she'd had the guts to say more.

Slumping forward, she rested her forehead against the canvas, not caring about the oil paint imprint. She'd never felt so alone, so defeated…and in the midst of her absolute misery a thought so profound, so awful, pierced her gloom.

What had she thought a few seconds ago? Something about making her *love* him?

She *loved* him? Was she out of her mind?

No way. It must be the stress sending her loopy. She'd heard about people going crazy with Post Traumatic Stress Disorder. Maybe her bout had set in early?

She couldn't love him.

He was cocky, self-centred, and a heartless businessman. He had insinuated his way into her life and got under her skin before flaying it with cold, calculated precision, all in the name of sealing his precious deal.

The very idea she could love a guy like that was preposterous.

But what if you do?

"Hell," she muttered, sitting bolt upright and staring blankly at the vivid canvas, wishing she could turn the clock back a few minutes and wipe out her insane thoughts.

Because once her stupid inner self had raised the possibility, she knew without a doubt the truth would destroy her and she wanted to head-bang the canvas repeatedly in the hope it would knock some sense into her.

"*Bella*, are you here?"

Ariel hadn't heard the chimes signalling Sofia's entrance into the gallery—the fault of her insane inner voice whispering crazy stuff about loving Cooper Vance—and she wasn't in the mood for a chat.

Maybe if she pleaded a headache she could get rid of her friend, close up for the day, and harass some poor courier to deliver a bomb along with the signed papers to Cooper?

Thanks to him, she had no option but to sign his stupid proposal courtesy of his traitorous deadline.

"I'm in the studio, Sofia," she called out, cleaning her brushes and palette out of habit rather than a driving necessity to do so.

Besides, she needed something to do with her hands other than put the finishing flourish on the document signalling her ultimate demise.

"There you are, my beautiful girl." Sofia bustled into the studio, dressed in head to toe fuchsia and sporting a hat boasting massive feathers that could take out a person's eye at twenty paces. "How are you?"

Ariel turned from the sink and rubbed her hands down the front of her smock. "I have a headache."

To her surprise, Sofia laughed rather than cooed in concern. "Must be all that paint seeping into your brain," she said, pointing to Ariel's forehead and grinning, her perfectly capped teeth in stark contrast to the bright pink of her dress.

Ariel managed a rueful smile as she picked up a nearby rag and swiped at her forehead. "I forgot in all the excitement."

"Excitement?" Sofia's nose twitched at the faintest hint of gossip usually and, like a rabbit sensing a juicy carrot, her nostrils quivered.

"Yes, the excitement of trying out a new technique. I

read about a tribe in Africa who only paint with their heads so thought I'd try it. Want to see the results?"

Ariel's grin broadened at Sofia's confusion. In a way, Sofia's impromptu visit had achieved a miracle already. She'd smiled, when a few minutes earlier it had felt like she'd never smile again.

"What on earth is that?" Sofia's hands flew to her mouth as she stared at the canvas, her shocked gaze darting between the painting to Ariel's face and back again.

"You don't like it?"

"It's horrible." She tut-tutted. "It's nasty. Angry. Ugly." She waggled her finger. "No, no, no, this is not you at all."

Ariel stood alongside Sofia and stared at the canvas, the vivid streaks of red, black, and yellow telling an emotional story she couldn't hide.

"I take it you don't want to buy this one for your collection?" Ariel asked, slightly embarrassed as she cast a critical eye over the painting. Usually, she expressed herself through her art, a way to feel good about the world, a cathartic experience. But seeing the angry slashes of vibrant paint saddened her and reminded her exactly why she'd picked up the brush on the return from Cooper's office.

She'd needed to debrief, to off-load, to express the devastation wreaking havoc on her psyche and painting had been her only option. Sadly, it hadn't helped, and now she had to allay Sofia's qualms before she blurted the whole sorry tale to her friend.

"What is it, *bella*? What is the problem?" Sofia grabbed her hands and squeezed, her coal-black eyes beseeching, a frown creasing her brow.

"No problem," Ariel said, using every ounce of self control not to fall into Sofia's arms like a babbling mess.

"Is it money? You need more than what the commission brought you? I can give it to you right now." Sofia released her hands to scramble in her handbag for the cheque book Ariel knew she always kept on her 'in case of a bargain'. Nobody used cheques these days but Sofia was old school—cash was king, apparently—and credit cards were for suckers.

Ariel laid a hand on Sofia's arm, stilling the scrambling woman. "I don't need money," *I need a miracle*, "but thanks for offering."

"You sure?" Sofia didn't appear reassured, studying Ariel's face with an intensity that bordered on uncomfortable.

"I'm sure."

Ariel could never ask Sofia for the money to buy out the lease on the gallery. She would never risk their precious friendship over a loan she had no way of repaying.

Aunt Barb had taught her many things, one of them being never borrow more than you can repay, and she'd adhered to that policy her entire life; which explained why she didn't own a car, had no mortgage, and paid her rent on time most months.

Until now.

"Okay. In that case, I dropped by to invite you over for dinner tomorrow night." Sofia paused, and Ariel didn't like her sly grin. "And I thought you might like to bring that delightful young man of yours. He likes lasagna?"

"No!"

"No?"

Ariel calmed her voice with effort. "What I mean is, Cooper isn't my young man. He's busy with work and I'm busy here, so we won't be seeing much of each other anymore."

Try never. Which would be too soon for her.

Sofia's mouth drooped in disappointment. "What a shame. Cooper is a nice boy. Excellent manners, such class, so handsome."

Nice boy? Ariel tried not to choke on the lump of disgust lodged in her throat.

"Aah...now I understand." Sofia pointed at the painting and grimaced. "You are very sad about not seeing him anymore. You love him and you are pining for him. It all makes sense now."

"I don't love him."

The moment the denial left her lips, Ariel knew losing the gallery didn't make her want to weep as much as the thought of losing Cooper.

For once, Sofia didn't push or probe or offer a ten minute matchmaking lecture. "Don't worry, *bella*. It will all work out in the end."

As Sofia wrapped her in a smothering hug, Ariel seriously doubted it.

Chapter Thirty-Three

Cooper paced outside the entrance to the National Gallery, oblivious to the stunning fountains, the impressive lead-light windows, and the natural beauty of the Royal Botanic Gardens opposite.

He had a lot on his mind; namely, the appearance of one stubborn, gorgeous artist and whether she'd give him a chance to explain.

It all seemed so clear after he'd sorted things out with his dad and he hadn't wasted a second in putting his plan into action. He just hoped the wheels in motion wouldn't be derailed by the fiery blonde harridan who had captured his heart without trying.

At that moment, he saw Ariel alight from a tram on St. Kilda Road and he exhaled in relief.

She came.

Then again, she would have, considering she thought she was meeting a representative of the Victorian Arts Council rather than the selfish brat she'd accused him of being earlier today.

His pulse raced and his heart turned over as she waited

THE CHARMER

at the traffic lights, a stunning figure in crazy striped knickerbockers, a flowing purple top, and towering cork wedges that tied around her ankles with black satin ribbon. The eclectic mix would've looked silly on any other woman. On Ariel, it looked amazing.

She had an inner grace, a special glow that made anything she wore or anything around her take on special significance, and he'd been crazy enough to almost let her slip through his fingers.

Thankfully, he'd come to his senses. Now, if only she'd give him a chance to prove exactly how much she meant to him.

Cooper waited in the lengthening shadows as early dusk fell over Melbourne, watching Ariel's every step with increasing impatience.

This had to work.

* * *

Ariel glanced at her watch as she reached the entrance to the Gallery, relieved to see she'd made it with a minute to spare.

This could be it, her one and only chance to save *Colour by Dreams*, and a golden opportunity to rip up the document burning a hole in her bag; the signed document she hadn't couriered to Cooper when the summons from the Arts Council's director's had arrived.

She hadn't questioned the timely request. She preferred to see it as a sign from the big guy upstairs that her luck had changed for the better. Besides, the director had been at Chelsea's showing and maybe he wanted to discuss the future of Victorian art and the part she—and her gallery—could play in it.

She closed her eyes and made a fervent wish she was right in her assumptions. However, when she opened them again and found herself staring into Cooper's too-blue eyes, she knew that wishes didn't come true. At least, not for her.

"What are you doing here?" She spat out, gripping her bag tightly to prevent herself from swinging it at him, her first crazy impulse when she saw his handsome face.

"There's something you should see inside," he said, his well-modulated voice raising her hackles.

Why couldn't he be more ruffled, more scruffy, less polite, less perfect? She felt gauche, unworldly, and flawed next to him, and she hated it. If his mere presence here hadn't undermined her, his air of cool unflappability would have.

She stuck a hand on her hip and tossed him an 'I don't give a damn' look. "What's this something I need to see? A picture of you in all your smug glory because you've won?"

She paused and tapped her lip with a chewed fingernail, as if deep in thought. "Though that can't be right. As high as the Gallery ceilings are, I doubt they could fit a portrait of your big head in there."

To her chagrin, he didn't react, apart from a slight twitch at the corners of his mouth. That very kissable mouth, the same mouth that had worked its magic on her and coerced her into believing a lot of garbage, mainly that she loved him.

She had to be nuts.

"This will only take a few minutes." He held his hands out, palm up, like he had nothing to hide. "What have you got to lose?"

"Everything," she muttered, casting longing glances at the departing tram she'd just disembarked and shuffling uncertainly from foot to foot, before shrugging and making a beeline for the Gallery, not caring if Cooper fell into step beside her or not.

She waited until they entered the cool interior and moved away from the door before confronting him.

"The director's not coming, is he? This was another of your sick power plays to get me to jump to your tune."

A statement, not a question, because she already knew he'd do anything to get what he wanted, and she wondered why she'd followed him in here.

Because you love him.

Because you still harbour some crazy hope this is all a bad dream and you'll wake up to a perfect day.

Because you're creative and are way too good at building ridiculous fantasies of happily ever after in your head.

"No, the director isn't coming." The jerk had the grace to look sheepish. "I'm sorry about that. It was the only thing I could think of on the spur of the moment to get you here."

Anger made her fingers curl into fists. "What for? To rub my nose in it? To make sure I'd meet your stupid deadline?"

The silly thing was, he *was* rubbing her nose in it; rubbing her nose in the fact she loved him. Loved the way his blue eyes shone with intelligence, loved the way his mouth quirked when he struggled not to laugh, loved the way he filled out a suit, even if guys in fancy clothes didn't usually do it for her.

Ariel grabbed for a curl and twisted it around her finger, hoping the sharp tug on her scalp might erase her thoughts. Instead, it made her focus on Cooper even more as he reached out to still her hand before thinking better of it and lowering his arm to his side.

The truth—that she loved him, loved everything about him—made her choke up. Getting over Cooper would be yet another burden while she tried to recover from the loss of the gallery.

"I asked you here to give you this." He reached into the inside pocket of his silk-lined jacket and pulled out a folded document.

She cleared her throat. "Don't tell me. You've made another amendment to your proposal and demanded my soul as well."

He didn't flinch, didn't speak, but something about the hurt in his eyes made her feel lower than an ant's belly.

"Why don't you take a look?"

Rolling her eyes like an adolescent taking a lousy report from a teacher, she snatched the offending document and opened it, prepared to skim the print before folding it and flinging it back in his face.

However, her nasty intentions evaporated the minute her eyes focussed on the new owner of the gallery.

"What the—" She blinked and made a frantic grab at the recently released curl, winding it around her finger over and over, seeing the print but not quite believing it.

"It's yours," he said, shrugging his broad shoulders as if he purchased galleries for exorbitant amounts of money and bestowed them on needy artists every day.

She shook her head and read the final few lines of the document again, before lifting her head and staring at him in open-mouthed shock. "This is some kind of joke, right?"

"Of course not. I know how much the gallery means to you. This way, you won't have to worry about losing it ever again."

He spoke so calmly, so rationally, as if presenting her with sale papers for the gallery bearing her name as owner was nothing out of the ordinary.

"I don't get it." Ariel took a deep breath and exhaled

slowly, hoping the oxygen rush would clear her head. It didn't. She propped against a nearby wall, needing support at her back before she crumpled in an undignified heap.

If the realisation that she loved Cooper had her in a spin, it was nothing on the mind-numbing revelation that he'd bought the gallery for her.

The big question was why?

"I worked out a few things this afternoon and thought you'd appreciate the gesture." He shrugged. "As much as you want to deny it, I think we have a chance at being more than friends in the future and I wanted you to give us a chance without worrying about business stuff."

More than friends...

In an instant, the befuddled fog clouding Ariel's mind lifted and with a flash of blinding clarity, she knew exactly why Cooper had been so generous.

The resulting knowledge made her want to vomit.

"I'm not for sale," she said, each word uttered with icy precision as she handed him back the document that burned her fingertips with its treachery. "So we had sex? Big deal. It doesn't mean you can buy me for a few more cheap thrills. Nice to know what you think of me, though."

Anger flared in Cooper's eyes, sparking sapphire shards of fury. "Don't be ridiculous. I'm not trying to buy you. I just want this damn business sorted so we can get on with things."

"What things?" She kept her tone silky smooth when in reality she longed to knee him where it hurt the most.

He made a grab for her hands and she jerked away, his offer fluttering to the floor between them. "Don't pretend there's nothing between us. You feel the heat as much as I do. Is it so wrong to want to explore that further? To see whether there's a chance for a couple like us?"

Ariel wanted to run but couldn't move, trapped in the intensity of his stare, wishing he didn't have the power to make her pulse race and her heart turn over.

"There's no chance."

The knowledge stabbed her anew. They were too different, too conflicted, and his actions today spoke volumes. When the going got tough, he bought his way out of a situation.

For guys like Cooper Vance, money talked.

Unfortunately, she wouldn't listen. She couldn't. She'd learned long ago that no matter how desperate or hungry or cold, there had to be a line you shouldn't cross. Now, Cooper had unwittingly drawn that line and she wouldn't cross it.

If nothing else, she still had her pride.

She rummaged through her bag until she found what she was looking for. "Here. I think this is what you want."

She slapped the signed proposal in his hand and closed his fingers over it.

"This isn't what I want." Cooper shook his head and tried to give it back to her. "What I want is you."

Pain, fierce and deep, twisted her gut until she almost cried out with the agony of it. "Like I already said, I'm not for sale."

Without waiting a second longer, Ariel turned and walked towards the exit, praying her tears wouldn't turn to sobs before she made it out the front door.

"Ariel, wait!"

Ignoring Cooper's desperate plea, she picked up the pace, wishing she'd worn her ballet flats rather than three inch wedges today. That's all she needed, to break an ankle to match her broken heart.

"Please Ariel. I need you."

THE CHARMER

Her steps slowed as she reached the far end of the plush foyer, the front door in sight. She could've bolted for it, heels be damned. Instead, the moment Cooper laid a hand on her shoulder, she swivelled to face him, unsure whether to swing her bag at him or delve in it for a wad of tissues.

"What did you just say?" She tilted her head up, ignoring the tears pouring down her face as she eyeballed the jerk responsible for them.

"I need you." With infinite tenderness, he wiped the tears from her cheeks with his thumbs. "I need you. I want you. I can't imagine my life without you."

Once his thumbs stilled, he cupped her face, staring into her eyes like he meant every word.

As if.

Looked like he'd pulled out every weapon in his arsenal to win this contest. If he couldn't buy her, he'd schmooze her, just like he had from the very beginning.

"There's a word for what you're experiencing. Insanity."

"You think I'm crazy? Fine." He lowered his hands to clasp hers, holding on so tight her fingers tingled. "Tell me what you see."

His soft, husky tone took her back to the exact moment she'd asked him the same thing, his disappointing response, and the realisation at the time of the yawning gap between them.

The sad thing, nothing had changed since that day in the gallery when she'd done her best to show him what sort of a person she was, what was important to her.

Cooper only saw what he wanted to see and that would never change. For him, the world was black and white, a place filled with money and property and fancy cars, a world she could never belong or feel comfortable in no matter how serious his intentions.

"Let me go—"

"Tell me what you see." He squeezed her hands, his steady gaze never leaving hers for a second.

She rolled her eyes, knowing she had to put an end to this fiasco sooner rather than later. Her heart had already fragmented a few minutes ago when he'd thought he could buy her, no use letting it shatter altogether and do permanent damage to her insides.

"Fine. You want to know what I see? I see a big-headed, overconfident, pompous jerk who thinks he can buy everything he wants."

He didn't blink.

He didn't flinch.

Ariel found herself battling tears again at the cruel words she'd uttered in the name of severing ties with the guy she loved once and for all.

"Want to know what I see?"

"Not really." Her defiant act would've worked better if her breath didn't hitch and come out sounding like a pathetic sob.

"I'll tell you anyway."

To her amazement, he smiled, a gentle smile totally at odds with his usual confident grin and it almost undid her completely.

"I see a beautiful woman filled with fire and passion and conviction. A woman who gives her all to keep a promise. A woman who steals my breath away with how much I love her..." He trailed off and for a moment, Ariel wondered if her frazzled brain had conjured up the words she wanted to hear.

"Yeah, I love you. Go figure?" He tugged on their linked

hands and she leaned towards him, powerless to stop the swift, fierce kiss he slanted across her lips as if branding her as his.

"You love me?" She murmured, pulling back to stare at his face while wishing he'd kiss her again and again until she didn't have to think anymore.

He nodded, his blue eyes glowing with an emotion that could only be labelled love, its warmth radiating and infusing her with a bone-melting heat.

"I love every crazy bit of you, from that over-stressed curl you keep winding around your finger to the bottoms of those outlandish shoes you wear and every delicious inch in between." He placed a finger under her chin and tipped it up, his gaze drifting to her lips with the goofiest expression on his face. "I love you, Ariel Wallace. So what do you think about that?"

"I think you've been spending too much time at the studio and those paint fumes have affected you as much as they've affected me."

The corners of his delightful mouth twitched. "Does that mean—"

"Yeah, you lunatic. I love you too. Don't ask me why because we're as opposite as two people can get but somehow, I've fallen for you."

"Such words of love. Be still my beating heart." He grinned and placed her hand on his heart with his hand covering it.

Ariel grinned back, enjoying that his heart pumped as hard and fast as hers and wondering exactly how much more their respective organs could take when they moved past the kissing part onto the good stuff again.

"You know I'll still paint and run the gallery and wear funky fashion?"

He pressed his lips to hers in a slow, lingering kiss, the type of kiss that her melding to him, wishing their clothes would disappear, and they could find themselves miraculously in a private place.

"You know I'll still acquire land and develop properties and wear suits and ties?"

She shrugged, staring up at him from beneath her lashes. "I suppose I can learn to live with it."

"But can you learn to live with this?"

His hot, open-mouthed kiss had her hankering for more, a lifetime more.

Epilogue

"I now declare the *Barbara Vann Art School* officially open."

Sofia cut the thick, red ribbon stretched across the front of the new building with great aplomb, before spoiling her regal act by grabbing a glass of champagne from Chelsea and guzzling it.

Ariel chuckled and leaned back, content in the circle of Cooper's arms as they watched Sofia and Chelsea take charge of the milling crowd and guide them through the glass doors of the new school.

"You made this happen," she said, snuggling into her husband's arms as a cold gust of wind blew up Brunswick Street.

"We both did," Cooper murmured against her ear, hugging her tight as his hands skimmed the sensitive underside of her breasts and made her shiver more than any southerly wind.

She turned in the circle of his arms and looked up, amazed that the man staring down at her with stars in his eyes and a wide, content grin was her husband.

"You've done an incredible thing honouring Barb this way." He stroked her cheek with gentleness. "She would've been so proud of you."

Ariel blinked back sudden tears, remembering a morning many years earlier when a compassionate woman had taken pity on a down-and-out street kid. "She took a chance on me when no one else would." She managed a wan smile. "Barb saw something in me I never knew existed. I owe her so much."

A flicker of remorse shot through Cooper's eyes. "I had no idea about your past and how much the gallery meant to you. I hate how I came on so strong, pushing you relentlessly, forcing you to sell—"

"Shh..." She placed a finger on his lips, a shiver of delight rippling down her spine when he nibbled it. "That's old news. Look how far we've come."

He glanced around, noticed the crowd had moved inside, and pulled her into the shade of an old oak. "Tell me, Mrs. Vance. Exactly how far have we come?"

He kissed his way from her finger to her wrist and slid his lips up her arm until her head fell back, yearning for his masterful touch on the sensitive spot between her neck and collarbone.

"Ooh...we've come very far," she murmured, melting into his arms, knowing she'd never felt so safe, so treasured, as she did in his embrace.

A tooting horn disrupted their encounter and Ariel chuckled at the mortified expression on Cooper's face as he straightened.

"What? Don't big shots get caught making out with their wives?"

"I have a reputation in the business world to uphold,"

he said, aiming for a haughty expression that fell flat considering the smug smirk on his face.

"Yeah, you're a real tough guy," she said, gesturing towards the art school over her shoulder with her thumb. "Not only did you throw yourself wholeheartedly behind the new and improved *Colour by Dreams,* you find this delightful row of old terrace houses, pay the owners ten times what they're worth, and develop them into an art school for underprivileged kids in the area."

Cooper's warm, tender smile never failed to set her pulse racing. "Hey, it wasn't all me. My dad's a 'tough' guy too. After all, it was his idea to get *Vance Corporation's* employees volunteering down here once a week as part of their better-employee-relations policy."

Ariel noted the pride in Cooper's voice when he mentioned Eric and she couldn't be happier. She'd watched the two of them re-establish a strong father-son bond over the last few months and had been touched when Eric included her in a boys' weekend away when her husband and father-in-law had gone camping.

That weekend had been particularly poignant because listening to Eric's anecdotes—how Cooper had kicked a football through the back window of their house and broken a TV, how Cooper hid marshmallows in his room as a kid, how Cooper read under the covers late some nights that he fell asleep at school—she'd learned more about her amazing husband.

As Aunt Barb would've said, 'all's well that end's well.' Her surrogate aunt had never been short of a cliche or saying, one of the many things Ariel remembered on this special day when the art school dedicated to her aunt's memory opened.

"What are you thinking?" Cooper slid his hands around

her waist and locked hands behind her back, bringing their lower halves into tantalising contact and making her wonder how soon they could escape to the cosy confines of her studio, one of their favourite places for making love.

It had all started there, and thankfully, Cooper had agreed to pose for her again, completely naked this time, though she never quite got around to painting him. He had a way of distracting her that made every colour she'd ever imagined coalesce into brilliant, startling clarity as he took her to the stars and back every time.

Smiling at her adorable husband, she said, "I'm thinking you and I are one heck of a team, Mr. Big Shot."

"I love it when you call me names."

He proceeded to show her exactly how much.

If you enjoyed this book, please consider leaving a review.
Each review counts and helps new readers find Nicola's books.

Next in the **REDEEMING A BAD BOY** series is
THE BEST FRIEND.

Abby's on a mission.
Nail the shoot on a luxury Whitsunday island and launch her career into the stratosphere.

She's on track until her best friend and teen crush Judd shows up.

Judd, a famous wildlife photographer, has travelled the world for eight years so once this job is finished, settling in Sydney holds appeal.

But what if a scorching island fling with his best friend changes everything?

Abby and Judd know that crossing the line from friends to lovers is one giant screw-up waiting to happen.

Will they reveal their secret desires and ultimately find happiness?

Get THE BEST FRIEND now!

FREE book and more

SIGN UP TO NICOLA'S NEWSLETTER for a free book!

Read Nicola's feel-good romance **DID NOT FINISH**

Or her gothic suspense novels **THE RETREAT** and **THE HAVEN**

(The gothic prequel **THE RESIDENCE** is free!)

Try the **CARTWRIGHT BROTHERS** duo

FASCINATION

PERFECTION

The **WORKPLACE LIAISONS** duo

THE BOSS

THE CEO

The **ROMANCE CYNICS** duo

CUPID SEASON

SORRY SEASON

Try the **BASHFUL BRIDES** series

NOT THE MARRYING KIND

NOT THE ROMANTIC KIND

NOT THE DARING KIND

NOT THE DATING KIND

The **CREATIVE IN LOVE** series

THE GRUMPY GUY

THE SHY GUY

THE GOOD GUY

Try the **BOMBSHELLS** series

BEFORE (FREE!)

BRASH

BLUSH

BOLD

BAD

BOMBSHELLS BOXED SET

The **WORLD APART** series

WALKING THE LINE (FREE!)

CROSSING THE LINE

TOWING THE LINE

BLURRING THE LINE

WORLD APART BOXED SET

The **HOT ISLAND NIGHTS** duo
WICKED NIGHTS
WANTON NIGHTS

The **BOLLYWOOD BILLIONAIRES** series
FAKING IT
MAKING IT

The **LOOKING FOR LOVE** series
LUCKY LOVE
CRAZY LOVE

SAPPHIRES ARE A GUY'S BEST FRIEND
THE SECOND CHANCE GUY

Check out Nicola's website for a full list of her books.

And read her other romances as Nikki North.

'MILLIONAIRE IN THE CITY' series.
LUCKY
FANCY
FLIRTY
FOLLY
MADLY

Check out the **ESCAPE WITH ME** series.

DATE ME
TRUST ME
FORGIVE ME

Try the **LAW BREAKER** series
THE DEAL MAKER
THE CONTRACT BREAKER

About the Author

USA TODAY bestselling and multi-award winning author Nicola Marsh writes page-turning fiction to keep you up all night.

She's published 82 books and sold 8 million copies worldwide.

She currently writes contemporary romance and domestic suspense.

She's also a Waldenbooks, Bookscan, Amazon, iBooks and Barnes & Noble bestseller, a RBY (Romantic Book of the Year) and National Readers' Choice Award winner, and a multi-finalist for a number of awards including the Romantic Times Reviewers' Choice Award, HOLT Medallion, Booksellers' Best, Golden Quill, Laurel Wreath, and More than Magic.

A physiotherapist for thirteen years, she now adores writing full time, raising her two dashing young heroes, sharing fine food with family and friends, and her favorite, curling up with a good book!

Printed in Great Britain
by Amazon